P9-AZX-993

MASTER OF DECEIT

MASTER OF DECEIT

J. EDGAR HOOVER AND AMERICA IN THE AGE OF LIES

MARC ARONSON

CANDLEWICK PRESS

Image credits appear on page 220.

First edition 2012

Library of Congress Cataloging-in-Publication Data

Aronson, Marc.
Master of Deceit: J. Edgar Hoover and America in the age of lies / Marc Aronson. — 1st ed.
p. cm.
ISBN 978-0-7636-5025-4
1. Hoover, J. Edgar (John Edgar), 1895–1972—Juvenile literature. 2. United States. Federal Bureau of Investigation—Officials and employees—Biography. 3. Government executives—United States—Biography. 4. Police—United States—Biography—Juvenile literature. 5. United States—History—20th century—Juvenile literature. 6. Communism—United States—History—20th century—Juvenile literature.
I. Title.
HV7911.H6A76 2012
363.25092—dc23 [B] 2011046078

12 13 14 15 16 17 HMP 1 2 3 4 5 6 7 8 9 10

Printed in Castleton, NY, U.S.A.

This book was typeset in Utopia and Trixie.

Candlewick Press
99 Dover Street
Somerville, Massachusetts 02144

visit us at www.candlewick.com

TO LOUIS POST, RICHARD WRIGHT,
MARGARET CHASE SMITH, FRANK KAMENY,
AND THE MANY OTHERS WHO REFUSED TO BE
INTIMIDATED BY THE LEFT OR THE RIGHT
AND SPOKE THEIR OWN PERSONAL TRUTHS.
FEAR RULES ONLY SO LONG AS WE LET IT.

CONTENTS

PROLOGUE
Blackmail

FACT: In November 1964, William Sullivan, an assistant director of the FBI, set out to blackmail Dr. Martin Luther King Jr.

FACT: Sullivan was not only one of the highest-ranking FBI officers; he also had good reason to believe he would succeed J. Edgar Hoover as the head of the organization—if only he could overcome his terrible mistake of having once defended Dr. King.

THE INSIDE STORY: On November 24, an FBI agent boarded an airplane from Washington to Miami in order to mail a package. The box held audiotapes and an anonymous letter, probably written by Sullivan. "King," the letter warned, "there is only one thing left for you to do. You know what it is. . . . You are done. There is but one way out for you. You better take it before your filthy, abnormal, fraudulent self is bared to the nation." Though the letter was deliberately ambiguous about what "way out" Dr. King should take, King believed the note was telling him to commit suicide.

How could one of the most honored and trusted law officers in America conspire to destroy Dr. King? How could he imagine that blackmail leading to suicide was legal? Hoover, the longtime head of the FBI, was furious at King for criticizing his men. And he was certain that King was a pawn under Communist influence, which meant that he had to be exposed, marginalized, and neutralized. Stopping the "reds"—the Communists—was more important to Hoover than anything: laws, rights, even human lives. The plot against Dr. King opens a window into a dark past—a time of secrets and lies, an era when Hoover both protected America and betrayed the principles that define its system of government.

The plot against King was not a strange, onetime fluke. It was the product of a time when a branch of the government—our government—believed that its mission to defend against revolutionaries was more important than any law. This book is a journey back into that age of war and cold war, into the time that produced J. Edgar Hoover. Whenever America faces threats, there will be those who offer us security—at a price. That price may be your privacy or the freedom of a classmate or the life of a leader. We cannot know how we will react to the next crisis—but we can learn by revisiting, and reliving, the last one.

KING,

I will not dignify your name with either a Mr. or a Reverend or a Dr. And, your last name calls to mind only the type of King such as King Henry the VIII

King, look into your heart. You know you are a complete fraud and a great liability to all of us Negroes. White people in this country have enough frauds of their own but I am sure they don't have one at this time that is any where near your equal. You are no clergyman and you know it. I repeat you are a colossal fraud and an evil, vicious one at that. You could not believe in God Clearly you don't believe in any personal moral principles.

King, like all frauds your end is approaching. You could have been our greatest leader. You, even at an early age have turned out to be not a leader but a dissolute, abnormal moral imbecile. We will now have to depend on our older leaders like Wilkins a man of character and thank God we have others like him. But you are done. Your "honorary" degrees, your Nobel Prize (what a grim farce) and other awards will not save you. King, I repeat you are done.

No person can overcome facts, not even a fraud like yourself. I repeat - no person can argue successfully against facts. You are finished. And some of them to pretend to be ministers of the Gospel. Satan could not do more. What incredible evilness. King you are done.

The American public, the church organizations that have been helping - Protestant, Catholic and Jews will know you for what you are - an evil, abnormal beast. So will others who have backed you. You are done.

King, there is only one thing left for you to do. You know what it is. You have just 34 days in which to do (this exact number has been selected for a specific reason, it has definite practical significant. You are done. There is but one way out for you. You better take it before your filthy, abnormal fraudulent self is bared to the nation.

The FBI released this letter twice, selecting different words and sentences to black out. It has not explained the odd logic behind the choices. The second version can be seen on page 175.

LIBERATO

JANUARY 1919

20 CE

PART ONE

– NIKOLAI LENIN –

Nothing in This Book Matters Until You Care about Communism

The background image here comes from the same issue of the Liberator quoted on page 20.

The great Soviet director Sergey Eisenstein made this film based on John Reed's enthusiastic account of the Russian Revolution. For generations, Americans critical of capitalism found inspiration in Reed's life and his words.

1

JOHN REED AND REVOLUTION

Today, Americans face intense terrorist threats and thus hard choices: Which rights and freedoms can we, must we, curtail in order to be safer in our streets and homes? Can our government tap wires without a court order? Detain suspected enemies without specific charges? Subject members of one religious group to additional scrutiny at our borders? These are precisely the sorts of decisions that J. Edgar Hoover and his successors faced in dealing with Communism for much of the twentieth century, so there should be a great deal we could learn from reading about that time. But today, Communism and anti-Communism are just terms that appear on tests, like the Whig, Greenback, or Know-Nothing parties. Flattened out into a chronology of unfamiliar names and forgettable dates, the great dramas of the twentieth century are useless to us. We can benefit from the story of Communism and anti-Communism only if we experience it as the people who lived it did—with passion. Once you step inside the mind of that recent past, you will have a new tool for facing the challenges of our time.

THE TRUTH OF AMERICAN HISTORY

There are two ways to tell the story of America. Here's one: Yearning to be free, courageous individuals set out from England to the New World. From the *Mayflower* on, the spirit of this land has been that of liberty and personal effort. No longer needing to bow to kings or obey priests, Americans set out to improve themselves and to show the world what democracy, industry, and individual effort could achieve. America is the land where anyone can make good. We see that over and over again, from the farmers of the rocky soil of New England to the settlers hitching up their wagons to go west to the immigrants flocking to our shores to the intrepid businessmen who built the shops, factories, and corporations that made this land the wealthiest place in the world. America is proof that capitalism works: every person seeking his own fortune, aiming to "make it," can succeed.

Here's a second way to describe our past: As the Communists see it, what you have just read is a lie. America was settled by racists who murdered Indians, enslaved Africans, and silenced women. Every time the poor or the enslaved tried to rise up, they were either shot at or imprisoned. Worse yet, through the aid of the media, and with the cooperation of prosecutors, judges, and lawmakers, those heroes who fought for all Americans were called un-American. America's poor are kept docile by TV, games, and fast food; they are pigs at the trough, fed slop to keep them happy on the way to the slaughterhouse. As the journalist John Reed wrote in 1918, "Nothing teaches the American working class except hard times and repression. Hard times are coming, repression is organized on a grand scale." America is proof: in order for capitalists to get filthy rich, they must have a base of the divided, ignorant poor they can use. The future belongs to the people, united, working together for a future in which all share and all are equal.

It is nice to believe the first story. It feels good; you can feel proud to be an American and hopeful about the future. But if, having grown up with that patriotic tale, you began to see the holes in it—the land stolen from the Indians, the endless labor of the Africans, the strikes broken by Pinkertons hired by callous bosses, the illegal wiretapping and break-ins organized by the FBI—then the second story offers a thrilling clarity. It is like waking up from a dream: you suddenly understand the way America and indeed the world works. The author Arthur Koestler, who was a Communist for many years, described that moment perfectly: "New light seems to pour from all directions across the skull; the whole universe falls into pattern like the stray pieces of a jigsaw puzzle assembled by magic at one stroke." And you have a mission: you must bring this truth to the world; you must free your fellow Americans from their illusions. You must be the beacon of truth in a land of lies.

The first view celebrates individuals: the brave pioneer, the courageous immigrant, the brilliant inventor. A nation is great if it protects our right to make choices: to pray, to vote, to make money, to pass our property on to our children. In this view, the more freedom each one of us has, the better off we all are.

The second view turns those same beliefs upside down. The nineteenth-century German philosopher Karl Marx claimed that the tale of individual choice and progress was an illusion. The victims of society—the poor, working people, the enslaved, women, children—were prisoners of their condition. They were so crushed by their basic needs—to eat, to have shelter, to survive another day—that it was a cruel joke to speak about them as individuals who could improve their lot. All the fine talk about free enterprise and private initiative was like the false promise of the lottery: sure, one person may win the jackpot, but millions of players are sure to lose. Marx wanted to change the game so that everyone would be guaranteed to do somewhat better, even if that meant there were no big winners. Improving the lives of working people, the vast majority of suffering humanity, was all that mattered.

For workers seeking a way to change their lives of backbreaking toil, for idealists troubled by the vast gaps between rich and poor, by racism, and by the oppression of women, and for intellectuals drawn to sharp, skeptical analyses, Marx was a golden light in a dark world. And yet that is not the end of the story. Who exactly are "the people"? If the poor are downtrodden, uneducated, and ignorant, who speaks for them? What if most citizens prefer to go to church, or play with their children, rather than take over the government? Does that mean a small group can rule in the name of "the people"? If that is so — and, in fact, that is precisely how Communism has played out almost everywhere it has gained power — then who is the bigger liar: the capitalist who teases the poor with images of goods they cannot afford or the Communist who hypnotizes the masses with empty slogans and false ideals?

Communism upholds the ideal of helping the helpless — which has not worked out in practice. But what about capitalism? Are we really all that free? Are we able to hold any idea? Express any point of view? The Supreme Court has ruled that high schools and even colleges can censor school newspapers. How free is that? Political campaigns run on money, and those with plenty to spend make sure to drown every potential winner in lavish contributions. How can any individual swim against that tide? According to a recent survey, only 28 percent of high-school biology teachers in America follow the National Research Council's guidelines on how to teach evolution. Most of the other 72 percent are not creationists; they're just cowed, depriving their students of real science because they are too afraid of their own communities. And what if you begin to believe in Marx, if you think America needs to be totally and completely changed? Are you free to believe that? To argue for it? To organize for it? To plot and plan to bring about a revolution?

Communism is beautiful in theory, but Communist nations have murdered millions upon millions of their own citizens. Capitalism offers freedom while letting the wealthy and powerful set the rules. These are the competing visions that people struggled to judge in the twentieth century. Switching from one view to the other led some to spy for foreign governments, to betray their closest friends, and even to suffer mental breakdowns. And the questions of how we should live are still with us today. If the good life is buying a new Wii, the latest iPhone, or a game the day it's released, then America is a great place to be. If the good life is impossible until the system that rules us is changed, then these little treats are pathetic bribes and America is a prison. Is the truth in being just like everyone else or in demanding radical change? What should you do if everyone around you is blind to the truth? What should you do if you begin to doubt the truth you once believed in?

WHY NOT REVOLUTION?

How does change come to nations? For people who believe Marx, the answer is obvious. Those who have power will never give it up. Why would they? The rich have always staged lavish spectacles to distract the poor—how different is *American Idol* from *The Hunger Games*? Or they whip up fear and hatred of outsiders, so that workers do not recognize their real enemies. Notice how anti-immigrant talk spread after the 2007 economic crash. There may even be elections in which a candidate claims to be the voice of the neglected and abused. But that is one more illusion. The small class of people who control the economy of a nation are the real rulers, and they clutch on to power. The only way actual change comes is through force.

When the victims of the wealthy and powerful band together, throw off their chains, and seize control of the economy, that is the first and only moment of hope. The word *revolution* means "turning over," the world turned upside down: the worker drives off the boss and takes control of the factory; the students run the school; the hungry demand the bread they need. A revolution breaks the spell, and the vise grip, of the rich through the massed power of their victims. And so, just as in childbirth, the birth of a new society must come with blood. No one voluntarily gives up power, so those who recognize their oppression must train to seize control. Indeed, many revolutionaries do not shrink from violence; they believe that only bullets and bombs can bring liberation.

Violent revolution brings a thrilling clarity: no more compromises, no more lies, no more bending to old ways or old people—which makes it particularly appealing to the young. The English poet William Wordsworth described that feeling perfectly, because he felt it during the French

Completed in 1833, this classic painting by Jean-Victor Schnetz captures the combination of idealism and tragedy that can come with violent change, in this case the so-called July Revolution of 1830 in France.

Revolution: "we who were strong in love! / Bliss it was in that dawn to be alive, / But to be young was very heaven!"

Who believes in this idea of necessary violence? Certainly people like Marx. But Thomas Jefferson himself said exactly the same thing. In 1787 he wrote, "The tree of liberty must be refreshed from time to time with the blood of patriots and tyrants." The author of the Declaration of Independence, soon to be the third president of the United States, a Founding Father if there ever was one, announced the need for violent change.

When he first took office, Abraham Lincoln — the man most historians believe was the best president America ever had — added that whenever the people "shall grow weary of the existing Government, they can exercise their constitutional right of amending it or their revolutionary right to dismember or overthrow it." Revolution is not just a Communist idea, a Russian idea; it is bred in the bones of America.

But is revolutionary violence any different from a dictator's murders? Revolutionaries may say they love the people, but that does not mean they are any better leaders than the kings, emperors, and tsars who say God gave them the right to rule. Was the French Revolution, which made Wordsworth dizzy with happiness, the birth of a new and better world or of a heartless tyranny wrapped up in fine words? These questions are abstract and theoretical to us, but in 1917 they were the most practical choices.

OCTOBER 1917

John Reed was born in 1887 to a wealthy family in Portland, Oregon, and grew up to study at Harvard when the college was all male and overwhelmingly white, Protestant, and privileged. But Reed was hungry for new ideas and burned to change the world. Wherever he went, whether he was drinking with radical artists in New York's Greenwich Village or rushing off to Mexico to write about revolution, he was a shining star. If there was a pulse of change in the world, Reed needed to be there to share the good news.

World War I began in 1914, and it sent ancient empires crashing into one another like tilting icebergs. Amid the gore and death, the world of kings and princes seemed to be destroying itself. In October 1917, Reed got word that he must dash off to Russia. There, he saw a tiny group of committed Communists take over the vast empire that the Romanov family had ruled for three hundred years. Led by Vladimir Lenin, the disciplined cell of revolutionaries named themselves Bolsheviks — the "majority" party — as if they were the true voice of Russia's toiling masses.

Reed described the Bolshevik takeover in his book *Ten Days That Shook the World.* Seeing the revolution unfold before him, he "suddenly realized that the devout Russian people no longer needed priests to pray them into heaven. On earth they were building a kingdom more bright than any heaven had to offer, and for which it was a glory to die." (Reed's experiences are vividly reenacted in *Reds,* the 1981 film about his life.)

The Soviet artist El Lissitzky created this design for an ultramodern movable tower from which Lenin could spread his new truths to the people.

This new kingdom was for the whole earth, not just Russia. "A great idea has triumphed," said one admiring American. The working people had their first victory, and Communists believed the whole world would soon follow.

Reed believed that the Russian Revolution was the beginning of a new era. For once, the poor had fought and had won. Now they ruled Russia, and they would make an example of that vast land. They would show the path to the future for working people everywhere. To those idealists, the message of Russia in 1917 was hope. No government was safe. Soon the laborers who worked endless hours in soulless factories would rule the world.

In 1917, just as Reed was in Russia basking in the glories of the revolution, a young lawyer named John Edgar Hoover was beginning to burrow his way into the heart of the American government, in Washington, DC.

2

THE RISE OF J. EDGAR HOOVER: THE FIRST SECRET

If you took everything about John Reed and reversed it, you would just about have J. Edgar Hoover. Reed was a charismatic star of Greenwich Village at its wildest, and he was free to be radical because he was rich. From an early age, he was eager to taste life—having affairs with women, seeking adventures overseas, marching alongside striking workers. People noticed Reed, who was so willing to upset conventional Americans that many saw him as "'wild' and 'crazy' and 'irresponsible.'" When he wasn't ablaze with some new radical activity, he was writing poems and plays to preach revolution. Hoover, on the other hand, was born in 1895 in a modest home in a modest section of Washington, DC. He lived in his family home until he was in his forties and his mother passed away. As a teenager, he was an ace student in Sunday school, and he attended church throughout his life. In school, Hoover won contests for his debate team by citing the Bible and the example of "Christian nations" to defend capital punishment. He never left the United States, never married, did not date, and, in all likelihood, never had a sexual relationship with anyone (more on this later).

Reed was most at home in mixture; he needed to be where men and women, rich and poor, black and white, American and Russian flirted, argued, and plotted to change the world. Hoover loved marching in the school cadet corps and was such an upstanding young man that he would teach Sunday school wearing his cadet uniform — the very picture of knife-edged creases, firm rules, and accepted moral values. Being a cadet was more than wearing a uniform; it fit his preference for separation and conformity. Hoover loved being around guys, being in an all-male club with his very special friends. As he was about to graduate from high school, he wrote that "the saddest moment of the year was when I realized that I must part with a group of fellows who had become a part of my life." He needed a "group of fellows" around him all the time. And, having grown up in a totally segregated Washington, attending all-white schools and churches, he was deeply alarmed at the idea of racial mixture. If we look back to the two versions of American history, Hoover never wavered in believing the first, while Reed devoted his life to the second.

And yet it is not hard to see that the crisp, firm face Hoover presented to the world was the product of steely determination and unceasing vigilance. As a child, Hoover was short, somewhat overweight, and he stuttered. He overcame these challenges by pure will. He discovered that if he spoke quickly, he could outrace his stutter, so night after night he practiced speaking until he was good enough to become captain of the debating team. From then on he always spat out his words rapidly with a machine-gun rat-a-tat-tat of hard facts and firm judgments.

Hoover as a cadet, displaying his knife-edged precision and unwavering moral severity. Though the date of the photo is unknown, he is somewhere between sixteen and eighteen years old.

Seated holding flowers and smiling to himself, Hoover at twelve gives a hint of his taste for performing.

Later in life, when people began to write his official biographies, he made up stories highlighting his supposed childhood athletic skills. Whether by training himself or shaping how he was described, Hoover controlled the story: you learned only what he wanted you to know.

Does Hoover's stutter tell us something? While the problem itself may have been a genetic accident, the way he dealt with it opens a crack into the hidden chambers of his family life. Throughout his life, he was determined to hide all signs of weakness, and he became a gifted performer—always onstage, always selling the story he wanted you to believe. Most probably Hoover's need to seem perfect was related to the first secret: the tension between his stern mother and withdrawn father that he experienced every night.

THE ONE WOMAN HOOVER EVER LOVED

Annie Scheitlin, Hoover's mother, grew up in a nineteenth-century Washington family that was wealthy enough to educate her in Switzerland and was proud of ancestors who had been diplomats and colonial soldiers. She

Anne Schetlin Hoover, the stern, ambitious backbone of the Hoover household

carried on those military traditions, for she was known to be "a very forceful kind of person" who "made herself felt." Her marriage to Dickerson Hoover, though, disappointed her. Dickerson earned a limited income as a government mapmaker. Born in an era when intelligent, determined women had very few opportunities, Annie focused all of her frustrated ambition on her third child, whom she always called Edgar.

Annie and Dickerson's first two children were teenagers when J. Edgar was born, and she could see that neither of them was going to be her shining star. That left the newborn. The house was divided in two. On one side were the quiet father and the first two children: Dickerson Jr., an easygoing athlete, and Lillian, a rebellious teenager. On the other side were Annie and Edgar. Annie's rule was absolute: obey her laws, live an orderly life, and if you slip, expect punishment. Annie demanded order and excellence; Edgar eagerly accepted the challenge. As one niece recalled, Annie "always expected that J.E. was going to be successful." She "pushed" him "as much as she could."

The team Annie and Edgar formed during his childhood lasted the rest of her life. Like an attentive wife, Annie "ran a beautiful home for him." That did not mean they always got along. Known as two "very strong personalities," they clashed nightly over decisions as seemingly silly as how high to open the window shades. But that was the friction of two totally committed partners. Cartha DeLoach, one of Hoover's longest-serving and most loyal FBI colleagues, believed that Annie was "the only person for whom he held a deep and abiding affection."

J. Edgar and his parents, Dickerson and Anne

Hoover as a guy among guys watching a ball game; the four men seated around him are FBI colleagues. Hoover seems relaxed and happy.

One way to see young Edgar is as the favorite — molded and doted on but also smothered by his fiercely determined mom. But there was another side to him and to the Hoover family. They loved to go to shows, to see vaudeville acts. In the thousands of photos preserved in Hoover's personal FBI files, the shots taken at sporting events stand out: he looks relaxed, happy, and at ease — totally unlike the endless dour images of him taken in the office. As a spectator, Hoover came alive. But he was also a gifted performer himself. Young Hoover was always displaying something to the world, whether in the two-page local newspaper he created as a boy, the debates he won, the Sunday-school classes he taught, or the marching-band contests in which he excelled. Whether to please his stern mom or to enjoy his own power of persuasion, Hoover was always acting, always broadcasting his story, always on display.

While Annie was a partner to Edgar, his father was a warning to him. Dickerson's fragile state was one reason Edgar was so secretive, calculating, and ever vigilant.

When Edgar was eighteen, Dickerson began to withdraw into himself. He would be silent for long periods, then suddenly fearful. The Hoovers did not want anyone, even their relatives, to know. A visiting doctor sent Dickerson to a mental hospital, and he came out a ghost of a man. From that point on, Edgar shared a home with his haunted father and a fierce, frustrated woman.

Hoover at twenty-four—a handsome young man working his way up in government

Even in his weakened state, Dickerson managed to keep going to the office. But in 1917, four years into his illness, he was sent home with a note telling him to leave his desk by the end of the week and not come back. After forty years of loyal work, he received not a single penny of retirement pay or pension. Edgar kept that letter throughout his life. He had seen how power worked: if you showed weakness, you could be cut off instantly.

When Dickerson lost his job and retreated into himself, Edgar needed to step forward. He had been working his way up at the Library of Congress—throughout his life, he showed genius at creating, mining, and manipulating files. At night, he attended George Washington University, where he was studying law. He graduated from GWU in 1916 and earned his master's in law the following year. So in 1917 he was ready to help his family by starting a career in the Justice Department. That is where Hoover was working two years later when bombs exploded in Washington. Someone was trying to start a revolution in America.

3

"THERE WILL HAVE TO BE BLOODSHED"

At eleven p.m. on June 2, 1919, terrorists unleashed their fury at America. In key cities across the eastern United States, nine large bombs, each made up of at least twenty pounds of explosives, shattered glass and smashed wood. The Washington bomb blasted a quiet street that was home to one former and three future presidents (William Howard Taft, Warren G. Harding, Franklin D. Roosevelt, and Dwight D. Eisenhower). It was placed directly at the door of the chief law officer in the land, Attorney General Mitchell Palmer. Amid the splinters and shards — designed to maim or kill Mitchell, his wife, and their teenage daughter — Mitchell found a note carrying the credo of the bombers: "We have been dreaming of freedom, we have aspired to a better world, and you jailed us, you clubbed us, you deported us, you murdered us whenever you could. . . . There will have to be bloodshed. We will not dodge; there will have to be murder; we will kill because it is necessary; there will have to be destruction; we will destroy to rid the world of your tyrannical institutions."

Attorney General Mitchell Palmer's home just after it was bombed. This photograph appears to have been altered—note the shadows around several men in the foreground. Who did this, or why, remains a mystery.

While America was fighting World War I, it had been illegal to go on strike. Now that the war was over, some four million Americans from coast to coast were stopping work to demand—what? Better wages or a different system of government? The strikes and the bombing suggested to some—radicals and conservatives alike—that America was about to go the way of Russia and plunge into the fires of revolution. Indeed, two months earlier, in April, violent revolutionaries had put together thirty-six packages and carefully taken them to the post office. Each box was a booby-trapped bomb loaded with both explosives and acid. The seeming gifts were addressed to a mayor, a judge, a senator, a businessman, and others considered class enemies. That plot largely failed: the bombers did not put enough postage on all the packages, and after one box was opened accidentally, many of the others were intercepted.

Just over a year after the June attacks, on September 16, 1920, the bombers achieved their greatest success. A horse-drawn cart pulled to a stop on the corner of Wall and Broad Streets in New York, in the heart of the heart of capitalism: Wall Street. The cart erupted. It was filled with so much explosive material and so many heavy weights—designed to spread the carnage—that all that was ever recovered of the horses were two hooves and horseshoes. Forty people died in that blast, and hundreds were injured.

Someone speaking in the name of the people, the workers, the oppressed, was trying to start a revolution in America by murdering, or terrorizing, the power elite. From the radicals' point of view, the tree of liberty was getting a needed rain shower. Indeed, the January 1919 issue of the *Liberator,* a magazine published in New York by American radicals, featured a letter to "American Workingmen" directly from Lenin himself. "A successful revolution," he preached, "is inconceivable unless it breaks the resistance of the exploiting class. . . . We are certain that we are invincible." If you were a worker angry about your poverty and the conditions in your factory, if you were an intellectual drawn to Marx's ideas and inspired by John Reed's writings, Lenin was telling you that you would have to fight, bleed, and die. But soon enough your cause would triumph.

The shattered cart and scattered wreckage give a sense of the power of the terrorist bomb that exploded on Wall Street in 1920.

Attorney General Palmer knew what to do. Even on that June night as he held his sobbing daughter in his arms and stared at the wreckage caused by the bomb designed to maim or kill her, he forged a plan. He must locate and smother every radical threat—letting lawyers and judges worry about legality later. Fear and rage guided him, as well as a canny political sense that being strong in a crisis, defeating a terrorist enemy, could get him elected as the next president. "Palmer," a legislator assured him, "ask for what you want and you will get it. The government is behind you in whatever you do to root out this kind of revolutionary organization in this country."

PALMER'S RIGHT-HAND MAN

Capturing the criminals who had sent a man with dynamite to his own doorway was only the first step. Palmer needed to calm the nation by eliminating the larger threat to every sleeping child. He was not sure exactly who had planted the bombs, but he had a very good general sense. Communists who agreed with Lenin, anarchists who wanted to destroy all governments, immigrants from Russia who did not cherish America's laws and traditions—he knew how to find them. The endless waves of new arrivals to America had stopped during the war. But now every ship brought more people Palmer did not like and did not trust. Could it be coincidence that the strikes and bombs came just as immigration heated up again? Somewhere in that un-American mob, he was sure, lurked the terrorists.

Finding people whose views matched the piece of paper that came with the bomb was easy. But Palmer faced a legal problem: free speech is protected under the Constitution. The editors of the *Liberator* were free to read, write, publish, and sell books filled with Communist ideas. So while Palmer could quickly find American Communists, there was not much he could do about them. But immigrants without American citizenship did not enjoy the same rights. So even while he sent policemen to sift for clues to the bombings, Palmer planned a much bigger roundup. First he would nab every immigrant in the country who was not a citizen and supported anarchism or Communism. Then he would deport these un-American threats somewhere, anywhere—across an ocean. In order to locate, detain, and ship off all those aliens, Palmer needed the help of a hardworking, dedicated patriot who would put security first. Fortunately, just the right person had made a name for himself in the Alien Enemy Bureau of the Justice Department and was aching to get that job: an ambitious young man who saw a sharp line between good and evil, American and alien, and whose only indulgence was a taste for dapper clothes: John Edgar Hoover.

On July 1, 1919, Hoover was promoted; he was now a special assistant to the attorney general. His job was to "make a study of subversive activities" in the country, and to suggest "what action can be taken in the field of prosecution." This was a perfect match of man and moment.

By 1920, 579 agents working for what was then called the Bureau of Investigations were combing the country for dangerous radicals. Each week the agents sent between six hundred and nine hundred reports back to the home office. To some, this storm of paper might have seemed like a chaotic blizzard, especially since many of the agents were untrained or incompetent. To Hoover it was an opportunity. He loved to compile lists and organize them into categories. Every person named in a report became the heading on a file card. Soon that card filled up with more bits of information: where that person lived, what groups he or she belonged to, whether he or she wrote for a newspaper or magazine. Then new files were started for those same groups, papers, and magazines. Within a year, Hoover's team had some one hundred thousand of these files lined up, sorted, and ready for use. Though he was born long before the age of the computer, he created a kind of national database.

Hoover's assistants checked the cards for cross-references the way a search engine now surfs the Internet for websites. Hoover mapped the network of people who might be radicals, looking carefully for the nodes—the neighborhoods, clubs, and publications—where they gathered. Through the slow, steady, relentless gathering of details, his interconnected files became a kind of information machine that could detect who might be a threat. This was a magnificent creation for an ambitious young man still in his twenties. But it was as dangerous as it was brilliant.

Hoover did not think that cleaning out the infection of dangerous immigrants was enough. He also had his eye on citizens; indeed, he believed that anyone who agreed with Lenin was a threat to the American government and the American people. Hoover saw what had happened in Russia—a tiny, very well organized group managed to topple an empire. He was determined that would not happen in America. For the rest of his life, he kept the Russian story in mind: no matter how few Communists there were, history showed they could have immense power—unless a ferocious defender defeated them at every turn. It was as simple as organizing a file: those who believed in revolution were, by definition, at least dangerous and very likely traitors.

According to the Russian calendar, the Communist triumph there took place in October (throughout the twentieth century, the phrase "October Days" meant the moment of revolution). But in the United States, the first anniversary of the Russian Revolution fell on November 7. Palmer and Hoover picked that as the perfect day to strike back against the revolutionary threat.

"WE'RE GOING BACK TO RUSSIA—THAT'S A FREE COUNTRY"

Around eight p.m. on November 7, 1919, Bureau of Investigations agents swarmed the Union of Russian Workers (URW) Building on East Fifteenth Street in Manhattan, where Mitchel Lavrowsky was in the middle of teaching a class. Born in Russia, where he was trained as a high-school teacher, Lavrowsky had later moved to New York, where he taught algebra and Russian at the URW. As Lavrowsky recalled, one man entered his class, pulled out a gun, ordered him to take off his glasses, hit him on the head, and pushed him down the stairs—where he was pummeled by other agents. Nicaoli Melikoff, who was a student at the Union, was searched by the Bureau men and robbed of a twenty-dollar bill. As he and other students filed out of their classroom, they were made to run between two officers who beat them, one by one. Nicaoli was the last one out, so he received special treatment: he was smashed to the floor and began to bleed. Then he was pushed down the stairs while being clubbed. Semeon Kravchuck, another student, was not even in the union building when the squad arrived, but he was heading that way. Seeing that, the officers ordered him inside, where they assaulted him and broke one of his teeth. Bloody, dazed, confused, everyone in the union building was then herded off to detention.

Why were these teachers and students brutalized by government agents? The union was founded by a Russian who then returned home to work for the Communists, and the organization quickly grew, spreading from city to city, serving as a voice for radical causes in America. URW halls were the perfect nodes on Hoover's file cards — places where potential threats to America gathered. But the union hall was also a school where Russian immigrants — who might not have the slightest interest in politics — went to take classes and improve themselves.

The raid left the inside of the union building looking as if it had been hit by a tornado: a scene of bloodstains, shattered banisters, broken glass, and smashed furniture. Some 211 students and teachers were rounded up for questioning, and not one was allowed to speak to a friend, family member, or lawyer. Lavrowsky was lucky: there was no reason to believe he wanted to overthrow the American government, so he was released at midnight. By four thirty in the morning, 171 others were also let go. That left thirty-nine certifiably radical immigrants, who were marched to the tip of Manhattan, to be ferried out to Ellis Island. For most immigrants, Ellis Island had been their entry into America. But for the thirty-nine it was the staging area for their deportation. As he walked toward the ferry, one shouted, "We're going back to Russia — that's a free country."

The next day, hundreds of New York City policemen spread across the city to round up more suspected immigrant radicals. In two days, more than a thousand people were taken into custody in New York alone. Despite the beatings, the late-night questions, and the atmosphere of fear, just seventy-five were finally determined to belong to a dangerous group, and only two — an Irish American and a native New Yorker — were charged with illegal support of violent politics. It was the same all over the country. In Hartford, Connecticut, one hundred men who spoke little English were nabbed. Week after week dragged by, and the detainees had little idea of why they had been taken in. Finally, after almost five months, lawyers managed to sort out which men were actually accused of being radicals and which simply did not speak English. All told, only 246 people captured in the raids were found to be so dangerous that they deserved to be forced out of the country. And yet Hoover and Palmer had good reason to believe that the night was a magnificent triumph.

The Bureau's agents cracked a counterfeiting cell in Newark; in Trenton they broke into what may have been a bomb factory (that all depends on whether the black metal spheres they found were actually bombs or were

The headquarters of the IWW (International Workers of the World) after a police raid in 1919. The IWW was a pro-worker, anti-capitalist organization similar to the URW.

intended to be used in the Italian bowling game of *bocce*), and in a Baltimore office of the union, they found their treasure: incendiary literature. A pamphlet in Russian urged workers to "convert small strikes into general ones; and convert the latter into an armed revolt of the laboring masses against capital and State. . . . We must mercilessly destroy all remains of governmental authority and class domination, liberating the prisoners, demolish prisons and police offices . . . shoot the most prominent military and police officers. . . . In the work of destruction we must be merciless."

To Palmer, this was proof: Communism was no mere theory; it was a traitorous plot to destroy the American way of life. Hoover made sure the newspapers printed the pamphlet, and the public responded. Most Americans were thrilled by the raids. They felt safer because tough, determined men like Mitchell Palmer were protecting them. Indeed, Palmer was looking more and more like the ideal Democratic Party candidate for the 1920 presidential race. Encouraged, Palmer and Hoover began planning for another, far larger, roundup for the beginning of the new year.

Political cartoonists caught, and whipped up, the national mood of anger at "foreign extremists"—a tone not very different from that shown in anti-Muslim jokes after the September 11, 2001, terrorist attacks.

5

LEGAL RIGHTS: HOOVER VS. LOUIS POST

What a birthday present! On January 1, 1920, Hoover would turn twenty-five; the next day the alien radicals would get what they deserved. Hoover's agents had spent the fall infiltrating meetings, joining clubs, and adding names to the card files. The moment an agent was sure someone was a dangerous radical, he filled out a warrant for the suspect's arrest—though he was not required to supply any proof. By the end of December, Hoover held more than 3,300 warrants. And he was about to arrest every one of these potential terrorists.

The vengeance of American law came suddenly and swiftly. On the second night of January, agents swept through thirty-nine cities and hauled in somewhere between five and six thousand people—there was no exact count. In Detroit, eight hundred men were detained in a windowless corridor with just one water fountain and one toilet. They had no food, unless a family member figured out where they were and brought it. But the detainees were not allowed to speak to anyone—neither relatives nor lawyers. Their confinement lasted six days. When the Detroit group was finally processed, it turned out that 350 of the detainees were either American citizens or could prove that they were blameless immigrants.

In Boston, it was worse. Six hundred people were jammed into a prison that had beds for half that number, and for the first three frigid New England winter days and nights, there was no heat. Not surprisingly, two of the suspects—which is all they were—contracted pneumonia; another killed himself by jumping out of a fourth-floor window.

Housed in prisons, corridors, or centers like Ellis Island, thousands of potential deportees were now in the government's control. There was just one problem: in the name of protecting liberty, agents had twisted, ignored, bent, and even broken the law. American citizens wanted protection from "merciless" terrorists, but they also expected that a person taken away from his home and family would get to find out why—and be able to plead his case in court. In mid-January, the government began the process of figuring out who they had captured and what evidence they actually had against them.

The key to Palmer's dragnet was the difference between the legal rights of American citizens and those who were not yet citizens. The Department of Labor oversaw immigrant issues at the time, and Palmer's team had found ready allies in that office. But when it came time to sort out the thousands of people being held in miserable conditions, the secretary of labor was at home, battling illness. That left his assistant, Louis F. Post, in charge. John Reed and Hoover were opposite personality types, but Post and Hoover had a different kind of clash: they had directly opposing views of the nature of rights and law. The two views of America were about to collide.

Hoover was pleased with the white, Protestant, male world in which he lived. In his mind, those segregated, insular streets were America at its best. His job was to identify and combat any threats to that happy homeland, and he took it very seriously. A diligent, thorough researcher, Hoover read all the Communist writings he could find. He knew exactly what Marx and Lenin advocated, on paper. To him, words predicted actions: Marx and Lenin spoke of the need for revolution. Communists believed in Marx and Lenin. So, he reasoned, Communists must be threats to the American government. Clearly, then, Communist immigrants did not belong in this country.

Louis Post in a photo taken around 1896. Born in New Jersey to a family that could trace its ancestry in America back to 1633, Post devoted his life to expanding opportunities for all Americans, regardless of their origin, skin color, or income.

Post grew up in New York City, traveled to South Carolina in 1871 to gather evidence against the Ku Klux Klan, and made his name in Chicago advocating for teachers and other workers. He was a product of an America of mixture and turmoil, where immigrants, blacks, and the poor were struggling to make their way. Post knew all about Marx and Communism, of course. But for him, deeds spoke louder than words. Radicals were always spouting off about revolution, anarchy, class war, and the like. That did not mean any of them, or the workers who stuffed their pamphlets into their pockets, were ready to take up arms. Post demanded careful and specific proof that an immigrant was actually plotting violent attacks before he was ready to deport anyone. In just his first month of reviewing cases, Post rejected more than two-thirds of the arrest warrants. Palmer was furious and went on the attack, using his allies in Congress to grill Post.

Confronted by suspicious representatives, Post was levelheaded, plainspoken, and all-American. He cut through the atmosphere of fear and made politicians who were ready to side with Palmer listen to common sense. "Are you a Communist?" one congressman asked. Post gave the perfect answer: Jefferson had been accused of being a radical, just as Lincoln was in his time. If you called someone an extremist, you put him in the best company.

Post's speech to Congress is the voice we must hear, even when we are filled with fear and consumed by suspicion. Every accused person—whether an American citizen or not—must know why he or she is in detention, be able to consult a lawyer, question witnesses who have spoken against him or her, and have a fair trial. Rounding up suspects and housing them for months in terrible conditions is un-American; speaking up for the rights of others is one of the nation's greatest, most basic, traditions.

Attorney General Palmer meeting the House Rules Committee to argue that Louis Post was in sympathy with America's enemies. He is the man seated to the far right at the edge of this damaged print.

Post's clarity and sanity won: Congress sided with him. He kept his job and went on reviewing the warrants Hoover's men had gathered. Eventually, 2,200 out of the 3,300 actual immigrants seized in January were let go. Ever alert to job security, Hoover could see that the mood in the country was shifting.

"HE'LL GET HIS YET"

Palmer had failed twice. First, he never found the original June 2 bombers who had attacked his own home. The only good witness the police tracked down threw himself out of a fourteenth-floor window even though he was under constant guard. The evidence gathered at that juncture pointed to a cell of Italians who hated all forms of government, not to Russians or Communists at all. The case was never solved. And second, Congress, judges, and the all-important court of public opinion sided with Post.

The public stopped believing in Palmer's campaign of fear and anger, especially when he predicted a new wave of violence and terror, which never took place. The Democratic Party thought better of having him as their candidate for president.

In his personal scrapbook, Hoover kept a photo of Post colored in with red pencil. Next to it he included a poem, which he may even have written: "The Bully Bolshevik," "disrespectfully dedicated to 'Comrade' Louie Post." Here are a few verses:

The "Reds" at Ellis Island
Are happy as can be
For Comrade Post at Washington
Is setting them all free.

They'll soon be raising hell again
In every city and town
To bring on Revolution
And the USA to down.

But Uncle Sam will clinch his fist
And rise up mighty strong
Take hold of Comrade "Louie"—
Send the "Reds" where they belong.
. . . .
But don't forget, he'll get his yet
For this is the land of the brave.

Hoover was canny. As he saw Palmer fading, he distanced himself from him. And when a new attorney general took office, Hoover knew just what to say. Harlan Stone—later a Supreme Court justice—was a reformer, horrified by the Palmer raids. Hoover so brilliantly convinced Stone that he shared those views that, in 1924, at the age of twenty-nine, Hoover was named head of the Bureau of Investigations. That is the job which, under various names, he would hold for the next forty-eight years—the rest of his life. Hoover had no doubt that the Russians were a real danger. Palmer's fall showed him that he would have to refine his tactics, pick his moment, and fight again.

PART TWO

turned a yellow rat
into the most dangerous
tommy-gunner
the world has ever known!

THE LEGEND: For thirty years, book after book, movie after movie, comic strip after comic strip told the story of how J. Edgar Hoover's efficient, relentless men tracked down and killed the ace bank robber John Dillinger. Hoover was so obsessed with the handsome criminal his men had gunned down that he displayed Dillinger's death mask outside his office. To meet Hoover, you had to pass the gangster's cold dead face.

THE FACTS: In the 1930s, movies and radio, national magazines, and syndicated gossip columns reached all across America. Hoover understood that in order to protect himself and gain new power, he needed relentless public relations. He really did create an efficient organization that killed or captured the most famous criminals of the Gangster Era. At the same time, he created an equally efficient organization to sell his—and only his—version of how that happened. If you opposed his story, or did not fit into it, Hoover would fight you every day of your life.

They are the EYES of America's No. 1 Gun-Moll

. . . *the woman behind the man behind the gun.*

The War of Images

...She's beautiful

...She's dangerous

...blasting her way from the amazing, true pages of J. Edgar Hoover's "PERSONS IN HIDING" ...the most sensational crime drama ever to explode on the screen!

J. EDGAR HOOVER
Director of Federal Bureau of Investigation

"Unquestionably top-of-the-bill quality from every angle. The real, authenticated article. All other previous excursions into this field have been ordinary 'cops-and-robbers' stuff." —*Hollywood Reporter*

adapted from J. EDGAR HOOVER'S "PERSONS IN HIDING"

LYNNE OVERMAN · PATRICIA MORISON · J. CARROL NAISH · JUDITH BARRETT

A Paramount Picture · Directed by LOUIS KING · Screen Play by William R. Lipman and Horace McCoy

Background photograph: Persons in Hiding *was a 1939 movie based on the official FBI version of the bloody rise and blazing fall of the bank robbers Bonnie Parker and Clyde Barrow.*

Tracer bullets used for night firing practice at the FBI training facility. Hoover put in place specialized training such as this to improve the skills and quality of his agents.

CLYDE: THE SECOND SECRET

In the 1920s, most experts believed that the American economy had turned a corner and clear sailing was ahead. Indeed, in 1929 a prestigious Yale professor announced that "stocks have reached what looks like a permanently high plateau." To many, the 1920s seemed to prove the optimistic, individualistic version of American history. More than any other place in the world, America could provide the goods, the income, and the opportunity people wanted.

Then, on Black Monday, October 28, 1929, the stock market crashed. The slide that began that autumn extended until the summer of 1932, by which time stocks had lost 90 percent of their value: a share that had cost one hundred dollars was now worth just ten. A man who enjoyed a good job in 1929, bought a car on credit, a home with a loan, and was building his family nest egg with ever-rising stocks was now out of work, standing on an endless line to cadge some free bread, or was so ashamed that he left his family to hobo around the country. His wife and kids scraped by.

Angry, hungry, scared Americans began looking for new answers. Perhaps the country needed a new kind of government, a new economic system. To many miserable Americans, even a bank robber seemed like a hero—a little guy striking back, taking what he needed. J. Edgar Hoover saw the despair and doubt of the Depression completely differently. First, a modern nation needed a modern investigation force—which he would build from the ground up. Then, second, he must convince the public that he was the man to guide these fearless, efficient lawmen. In order to do that, he needed to win three propaganda wars: making sure he was seen as tough and masculine; convincing the public to root for the FBI, not for glamorous bank robbers; and erasing the story of his own most famous agent.

BUILDING THE BUREAU

When Hoover took over at the Bureau, he faced a daunting task. The agency was a relic of a time of lax standards and small, ineffective national government. Some of his agents were corrupt; others owed their jobs to political connections rather than their crime-fighting skills. And they did not have very much to do. Agents rarely carried guns or made arrests, and they had no role at all in enforcing state laws. That left only cases that crossed state lines—federal cases—and there were very few laws covering such national crimes.

But Hoover had the energy, drive, and determination to create a modern, efficient organization. In 1924, he began gathering fingerprints from around the nation, and in the 1930s, he created a police lab and a training facility. He laid out clear, precise management rules and enforced them—even if it meant bitterly criticizing his most trusted officers. The men he handpicked were not the average cops on many local police forces or the shady private investigators the Bureau had employed in the past. Instead, his agents had legal training, would not take bribes, and were backed up by scientists and technicians who could find a clue invisible to others. The Bureau was Hoover's vision of logic, dedication, and order made real. He was like one of

Opposite: Hoover mapping the network of his offices and men. The map is a portrait of the national agency, linked by the clear chains of command he made possible.

St. Paul
Cleveland
Grand Rapids
Des Moines
Little Rock
Houston
New Orleans
Miami
Savannah

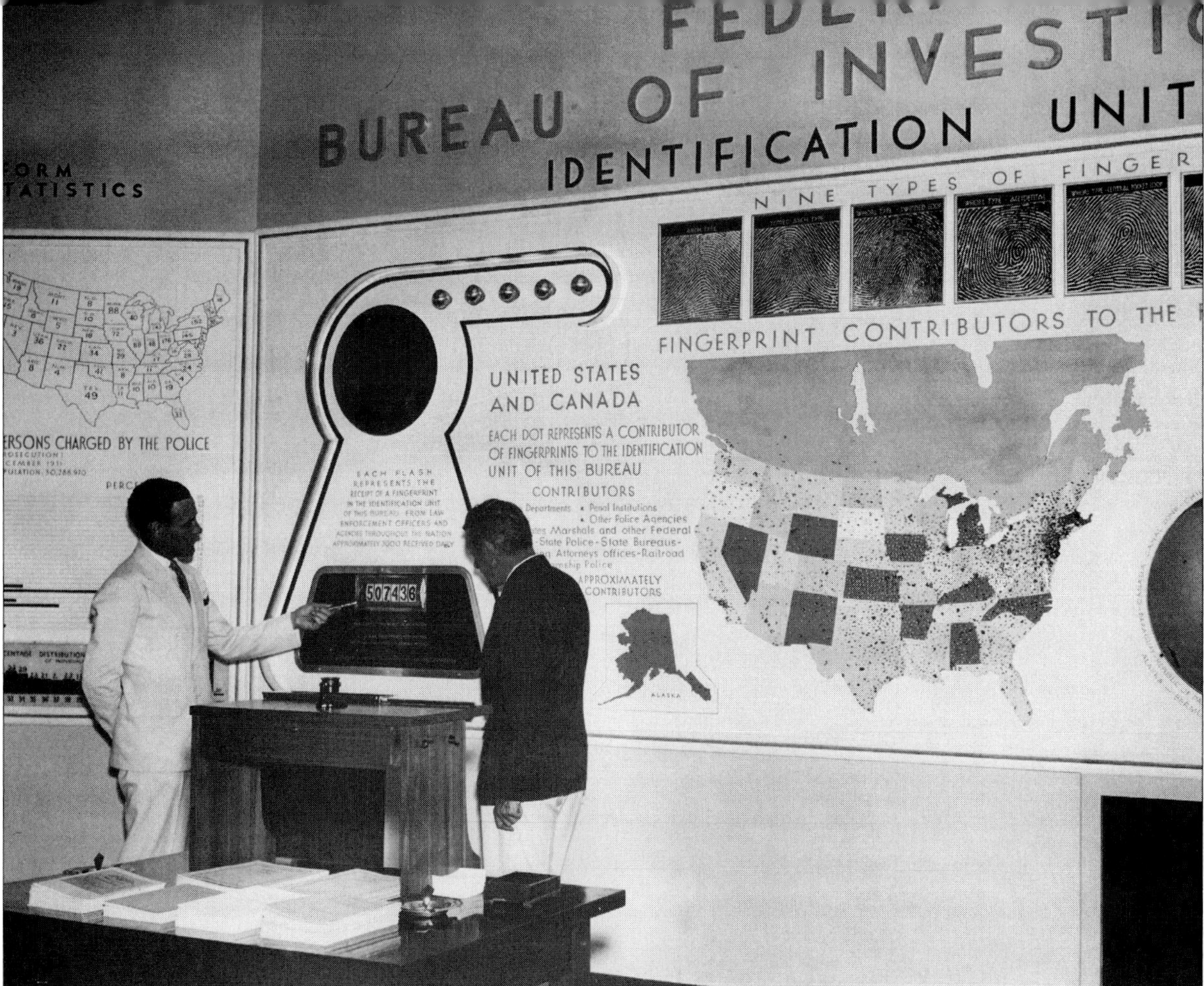

A national fingerprint collection perfectly suited Hoover's vision of law enforcement: scientific information gathered in well-organized files that allowed a small team of experts to catch criminals and protect the innocent.

the Founding Fathers, but instead of creating a nation and its Constitution, he built an agency to protect that country.

Nearly all the agents were men, and, at first, almost all were mainline Protestants. Later the FBI would become significantly Catholic and Mormon as well, with still only a very few Jews. Throughout the Hoover years, a trickle of black men were fully trained, accepted by their peers, and given responsibility for missions, but the agency remained almost entirely white until the 1960s. Hoover built the Bureau in his image of America and American values: upstanding, efficient, precise, uncompromising, familiar: a place where whites were at the center, men were men, and everybody knew the rules.

Hoover was married to the Bureau, which meant everything to him. That may be one reason he didn't want a wife or children. Work was his life and his family. Any involvement that asked more of him than routine and company would have felt like a subtraction to him; it would have taken him away from his first love: the agency he was building.

HOOVER'S SECOND SECRET?

Going after immigrant Communists with Mitchell Palmer had given Hoover his first break; battling gangsters now turned him into a hero. "The tougher the attacks get," Hoover boasted, "the tougher I get." That was his genius, dating back to his early childhood, when he mastered his stutter and triumphed at debate: his ability to turn every potential weakness into a greater show of strength. But that inner fire also exacted a price: his need to win was so powerful that it left a trail of victims. What drove Hoover? Why were power and control so all-important to him?

On March 1, 1932, the tiny son of the aviator-hero Charles Lindbergh was kidnapped and held for ransom. Two months later, the boy was found dead. The crime shocked the nation. Who would bring such a heartless criminal to justice? Local police did not seem to have any answers. Franklin D. Roosevelt had just been elected president but had not yet taken office. He had promised a New Deal in which scientific experts in Washington would manage the economy and lift the nation out of the Great Depression. Who could bring that same clear-eyed approach to police work? The *New York Times* reported that J. Edgar Hoover was a real-life Sherlock Holmes whose modern science and relentless determination could make the nation safe.

Or could he? An August 1933 issue of *Collier's* magazine described a totally different man. Hoover "looks utterly unlike the story-book sleuth. . . . He is short, fat, businesslike, and walks with mincing step." The word *mincing,* along with a description of Hoover's carefully matched tie, handkerchief, and socks, implied that he was homosexual. Was he? This is the second key question historians ask about Hoover.

Rumors about Hoover and men were common in his lifetime and are

Hoover was in his element in male clubs and secret societies. Here he accepts a "swagger stick" from the Potentate of the Aames Temple of the Shriners.

even more widespread today. The most frequently recounted myths are that he enjoyed wearing women's clothes, took part in homosexual orgies, and had a lifetime male sexual partner. The first two stories are simply not true. They say more about the fantasies and motivations of the people who spread them than about Hoover. Serious historians shade the third point in a more interesting way. Hoover loved being part of a close circle of guys—from his cadet corps to the Masonic lodge he joined to the Bureau he created. One astute historian calls this being "homosocial"—strongly preferring that all-male world. But he also needed to have one man in his life—one handsome friend to whom he was so close that they were inseparable. In 1928,

Clyde Tolson joined the Bureau and soon took the place of Frank Baughman, who married, and Guy Hottel, who was quite the ladies' man. For forty years, Hoover and Tolson left their separate homes and then rode to work, ate lunch, and vacationed together. In the 1930s they often wore identical clothes, as if they were kids playing twins at a dress-up party. Had Tolson not been so ill, he probably would have followed Hoover as the head of the FBI. He did inherit most of Hoover's considerable wealth. They were partners, but what did that mean? What happened between them in private?

In a photo album Hoover made for himself, he included shots of Tolson asleep in his pajamas, and a roll of pictures taken while they were on vacation includes an image of a fully clothed Tolson reclining on a beach chair at an angle that could be seen as intimate or erotic. But who snapped the pictures and whether they reflected humor, affection, or something more we just cannot say.

My view, and that of most historians, is that Hoover did not have a sexual relationship with Tolson. He was not hiding his bedchamber from public view. Rather, he was hiding his desires from himself. When asked why he never married, Hoover once said, "I have always held girls and women on a pedestal. If I ever marry and the girl fails me, ceases to love me, and our marriage is dissolved, it would ruin me. My mental status could not take it, and I would not be responsible for my actions." In his mind there was only purity and depravity—the pedestal or the raving lunatic. Even to feel desire for another man would totally unbalance his rigidly guarded "mental status." Having seen his father decline, he would never let that happen to him.

Hoover was obsessive, perhaps afraid of what he might find out about himself. Even though he washed, and washed, and kept washing his hands, he sensed that invisible germs and bugs were all around him and could easily invade his body. He added air filters to his house to "electrocute" poisons wafting by and built a special toilet seat, raised like a throne; that way, no stealthy microbes could enter him. But the dangers he sensed were not just viruses and bacteria; he was equally on guard against toxic ideas and emotions. Again and again he warned how evil forces could debauch, deprave, and pervert a child's innocent mind. As two leading scholars who have studied Hoover see it, Hoover devoted his life to building a wall against infections—whether those were germs, or desires, or Communists.

A new FBI agent was told to watch his words in the bathroom (where men might possibly try to match up with other men) because "the boss don't understand *queers,* but he's scared to death of them." Hoover was so afraid of being contaminated by homosexual desire that he, in a sense, spied on himself, making absolutely sure that he would never even feel anything shameful; he smothered himself. That mind-set also made him hyperalert to external threats. He lived in a constant state of suspicion—which is one description of just how alert the guardian of a nation's safety needs to be.

Hoover knew that even to dispute the *Collier's* article, which implied that he was homosexual, would be to spread the rumor. Instead, he made sure to take long, manly strides as he walked, and soon *Liberty* magazine announced that Hoover's "compact body, with the shoulders of a light heavyweight boxer, carries no ounce of extra weight—just 170 pounds of live, virile humanity." That was the Hoover strategy: don't argue with your enemy; create a new story that erases him from the record. The rumors about Hoover and Tolson were just one more threat that made him stronger.

PHOTO DOSSIER:
The following pages present a sample of the visual evidence we can use to make sense of Hoover, his inner desires, and his relationship with Clyde Tolson. Hoover was clearly making a statement about how similar he and his close associate were. Why? If you add together Hoover the lively spectator at sports events, Hoover the master filer, and Hoover the publicity hound, you get the sense that he liked display, performance, and watching others perform. Rather than being a person who needed to hide or disguise his private life, perhaps he just liked watching others and collecting their secrets while feeling safe and pure himself.

Above left: Hoover between Guy Hottel and Clyde Tolson, Miami, 1938. From his fancy shoes to the expression on his face, Hoover seems an almost giddy fashion plate—which could be interpreted as feminine.

Above right: Hoover and Tolson earlier the same year, demonstrating their identical manly determination—from the swing of their fists to the pace of their strides.

Left: Hoover and Tolson vacationing in Florida in 1937.

Above: Hoover and Tolson in their identical white suits, celebrating Clyde's twentieth year at the FBI

Opposite: This roll of shots taken in California, where Hoover and Tolson vacationed, might be seen as lovers' portraits, but we cannot say for sure who took them or what degree of intimacy they reflect. I found them among Hoover's FBI photo collection at the National Archives and Records Administration (NARA).

Below: This commissioned shot of Hoover's home shows him as the lifetime collector who loved getting presents and putting them on display. Equally evident are the statues of nude athletic males.

7

PUBLIC ENEMY NUMBER ONE: JOHN DILLINGER

In the early 1930s, America needed heroes. The glamour of the 1920s—Babe Ruth smashing home-run records, Charles Lindbergh soaring solo across the Atlantic, even so-called Captains of Industry and stock-market geniuses producing easy money out of nothing—seemed an outdated illusion. The most popular film in 1931 was *Frankenstein,* in which the main character becomes a savage beast. And the new star people rushed to see was James Cagney, playing a criminal on the rise in *The Public Enemy.*

People loved watching Cagney play a poor kid fighting his way up in a tough world where no one has clean hands. The film was fiction, but it was based on real gangsters of the time. The criminal with a gun and an attitude had become the new star. When one robber was caught, he spoke straight to those eager fans: "My conscience doesn't hurt me. I stole from bankers. They stole from the people." A gangster hero was Hoover's nightmare—until he seized the moment.

John Dillinger was a real-life Public Enemy who was as charming and fearless as any Hollywood star. He broke out of jail three times, and even when, as in this photo, he was surrounded by police, he seemed to be the one in charge, and sure of his next move. Sheriff Lillian Holley (on the far left) had Dillinger safely in her Indiana jail—until he made a fake pistol out of wood, grabbed real guns from his guards, and drove off in the sheriff's own car. The longer Dillinger was on the loose, the more he seemed like a dashing Robin Hood outclassing the fumbling, inept police.

This famous photo shows Dillinger, on the right, in complete command while in the hands of the law. Then as now, a person with star power could command a scene, even when under arrest.

Here is how Don Whitehead, in the officially approved book *The FBI Story,* described him: "John Herbert Dillinger led a kill-crazy gang which swept through the Midwest from September, 1933, until July, 1934." Dillinger's men robbed a dozen banks, then gunned down four lawmen in Kansas City. Hoover was furious. He saw the Kansas City Massacre as "a challenge to law and order and civilization itself." But in public relations terms, this "challenge" was just what Hoover needed.

Even as Dillinger was grabbing headlines, the attorney general was preparing a sweeping new anticrime program that granted Hoover and his men a vast array of new powers. The more Dillinger flouted the law, the more eager Congress was to arm and empower Hoover. Bureau agents were given oversight over newly defined national crimes; they could now make arrests and carry guns. Next step: bring down Dillinger, whom Hoover had dubbed "Public Enemy Number One." On March 31, 1934, two agents cornered Dillinger in a house in St. Paul, Minnesota — but they left one door unguarded, and he slipped away again.

MELVIN PURVIS

Dillinger's gang was loose somewhere in the Midwest. That meant the Bureau's team was going to be led by Melvin Purvis, a rail-thin, extremely short agent known for his South Carolina accent and his taste for just the right hats and clothes. Purvis was a dedicated lawman who had been promoted to be the special agent in charge in Chicago. Hoover and Purvis were quite different. The director was a master of filing whose genius was in running an organization, while his special agent worked best out on his own — even if that left his paperwork neglected and his staff confused. That difference in style was only the beginning of their fatal conflict.

Purvis learned that Dillinger and his men were squirreled away in a vacation lodge in Little Bohemia, Wisconsin. He rushed to phone Hoover, rounded up ten agents, and found two small planes (one borrowed from a movie actress) to fly them to a tiny airport fifty miles from the hideout. The

Bureau was still so small and ill equipped that the agent nearest to the airport was standing in the lot of a Ford dealership begging to borrow a few cars when he heard the planes overhead. In turn, Purvis had no plan: driven by the "fever for action," the agents were rushing to get to the Dillinger gang before they dispersed. While the airport was a scene of near chaos, back in Washington, Hoover was beaming. He was so sure they'd get the most wanted man in America, he couldn't wait to tell the press. Newsmen were told to be ready—the manhunt was just about to end.

By ten p.m., Purvis and his men were in the woods, creeping slowly and quietly toward their prey. Now they were just two hundred feet from the door. Suddenly the silence was broken by loud barking: two collies heard the men coming and were doing their guard-dog best to alert their owners. Sure that Dillinger would get the message and run, Purvis spread out his men and readied them to shoot. Three men came out of the two-story wooden lodge, settled into a car, and began driving, radio blaring, headlights off.

"Halt!" Purvis shouted. "We're federal officers!" The car drove straight ahead. "Stop the car!" yelled another agent. The car sped on.

Twenty-eight shots rang out—wounding two men, killing a third—and now, finally, warning the Dillinger gang inside. One after another they leaped through the back windows and scrambled into the dark woods. Baby Face Nelson was known to be a shoot-first heartless killer. As he was escaping, Nelson ran into two agents and a policeman. He killed one and wounded the other two.

Hoover's great raid, which he had hoped would be the triumph of his Bureau with its expanding role, left a dead civilian, a dead agent, and yet more proof that no one could touch Dillinger. Purvis offered his resignation, and rumors spread that Hoover might lose his job. Changing the headlines was now an absolute necessity. Hoover did not accept Purvis's resignation, perhaps calculating that to do so would be to admit that the Bureau had failed. But he appointed Samuel Cowley, another agent, to lead the Dillinger hunt.

During Hoover's lifetime, the official story never mentioned the innocent deaths at the vacation lodge; they were snipped out of history as if they had never happened. And that was just one of the many ways Hoover's public-relations men massaged the facts.

Since the whole Little Bohemia story had been erased, the official version needed a new starting point. Hoover's authors found just the right incident when Dillinger fled from Indiana to Illinois in a stolen car. Since the robber had crossed a state line, the Bureau was now on the case. This was perfect: instead of the agents fumbling an attack, they could be described as cool, efficient lawmen. Now Dillinger was the bumbler who did not realize the trouble he would bring on himself once he was up against the national organization. Hoover supposedly ordered Cowley to "stay on Dillinger. Go anywhere the trail takes you." Dillinger, though, had gotten a plastic surgeon to make him look like a different man. How was Cowley going to "stay on" a man who had become someone else?

As the old FBI story went, Cowley tracked down a woman named Anna Sage who knew exactly where to find Dillinger. The master robber was planning to take her to a movie the next day—only she was not sure which theater he'd choose. Cowley gathered a squad of agents and waited to spot Sage. Wherever she was, Dillinger would be. She wore an orange dress so she'd be easy to pick out. But under the glaring lights of the Biograph Theater, the dress looked red. The Woman in Red became the road sign. Once Cowley saw her, he phoned his boss, "who was pacing the library at his home in Washington." Purvis loitered at the front of the theater, holding a cigar, waiting for the most wanted criminal in America to emerge. When Purvis reached to light up, the agents knew they had their man. Dillinger sensed something was wrong, turned around, and saw a man walking toward him too quickly and purposefully. He "darted toward an alley, clawing a pistol from his pants pocket." The Bureau's men were a step ahead this time. "Slugs tore into Dillinger's body and he pitched on his face. The chase was over."

If you listened to Hoover, the success of the Dillinger fight was due to Cowley—who was soon promoted—as well as to the teamwork and efficiency of the Bureau. Purvis was there to help out and light a cigar. Unless you dug back in the archives, you would not know that the entire story was created to serve two purposes: to craft an image of Hoover's men as faceless,

WANTED

JOHN HERBERT DILLINGER

On June 23, 1934, HOMER S. CUMMINGS, Attorney General of the United States, under the authority vested in him by an act of Congress approved June 6, 1934, offered a reward of

$10,000.00

for the capture of John Herbert Dillinger or a reward of

$5,000.00

for information leading to the arrest of John Herbert Dillinger.

DESCRIPTION

Age, 31 years; Height, 5 feet 7-1/8 inches, Weight, 153 pounds; Build, medium; hair medium chestnut; Eyes, grey; Complexion, medium; Occupation, machinist; Marks and scars, 1/2 inch scar back left hand, scar middle upper lip, brown mole between eye-brows.

Hoover's pursuit of Dillinger aimed not only to capture a criminal but also to announce that a relentless and efficient set of lawmen was guarding the nation.

efficient, and irresistible, and to eclipse any memory of Melvin Purvis, superstar.

In reality, Purvis got the tip about the movie theater; it was part of a deal he'd made with Sage, an immigrant from Europe, who was in danger of being deported. She offered news of Dillinger in exchange for help staying in the country. Purvis promised to do his best. And it was Purvis who walked up behind Dillinger and insisted, "OK, Johnnie, drop your gun." While Purvis fought to make good on the deal with Sage, Hoover ignored him and made no effort to help her when she was deported. The clash over how to deal with Sage was just the first move in a larger struggle. Every time Purvis made the news, Hoover worked harder to overshadow him. By August, *American Detective Magazine* quoted Cowley as nominating a new hero in the Dillinger saga: "One man alone is responsible for the end of John Dillinger, and that man is J. Edgar Hoover."

While Hoover steered his press contacts to change history, he used his power within the Bureau to punish his all-too-famous agent. Purvis was criticized for being a poor office manager (which was true), for getting to work too late and not filling out forms correctly, even for speaking too softly on the phone. More than anything, Hoover was furious that Purvis seemed to like publicity, to want to call attention to himself.

In October, Purvis burst into the headlines again. He led a team of agents who trapped and killed another famous gangster: Charles "Pretty Boy" Floyd. Hoover immediately insisted that "Mr. Purvis is also to leave tonight and the curtain is to be pulled down on the publicity there." The curtain stayed down; reporters who asked the Bureau for the most basic background information on its star agent were turned away. Instead of being given juicy details about Purvis, they were instructed that "our system of operations is such that through cooperative efforts a case is broken." To call attention to any "so-called 'hero' of a situation" would only inspire jealousy and hurt morale. But Purvis just could not remain in the shadows.

On November 27, the Chicago office got word that Baby Face Nelson had been spotted speeding along on a nearby highway. Cowley and fellow agent Herman Hollis rushed to find him, insisting that Purvis remain behind.

That saved his life. A furious gun battle on Highway 12 left Hollis dead and Cowley mortally wounded. When Purvis got the terrible news, he raced to his colleague's bedside and swore, "If it's the last thing I do, I'll get Baby Face Nelson—dead or alive." Nelson was indeed soon found dead—from wounds received in the initial shoot-out. But that sensational vow—so perfect for the press—was also the end of Purvis's career.

The one man the press wanted suddenly became invisible. Hoover decreed that "he is not to come to the office." The missing man was demoted, taken off any case involving surviving members of the Dillinger gang, given unimportant jobs, and then, finally, transferred out of the Chicago office. Melvin Purvis was being erased from the Bureau. In July 1935, he resigned. But that made him much more dangerous to Hoover. As long as Purvis had worked for the Bureau, he could be muzzled. Now the media could have as much of him as it wanted. The war of images was going to be fought everywhere—from cereal boxes to movies—and only one hero would be left standing.

Purvis wrote the "inside story of America's most famous man-hunting organization" in a series of magazine articles, then a book; Gillette signed him up to sponsor razor blades, Dodge to promote cars. But his biggest score came on the breakfast table, where Post Toasties made him the center of their advertising campaign—complete with secret codes, a fingerprint kit, and a Junior G-Man badge, which in turn inspired Parker Brothers to create a board game called Melvin Purvis' "G"-Man Detective Game.

Post Toasties went all out in its Melvin Purvis campaign—offering kids badges and comics like this one, promoting a real-life detective hero.

Above: This short profile of Hoover appeared in 1935 and shows how his publicity minders wanted his story to be told. He was called Speed as a child, but that was because as a twelve-year-old, he started hustling for tips as a grocery-store delivery boy. His men generally did have training in both marksmanship and the law and had broken some spectacular kidnapping cases.

Opposite: Hoover on the set of the 1931 movie Little Caesar *with Edward G. Robinson*

J. Edgar Hoover struck back—brilliantly. First he used whispers, hinting to gossip columnists that Purvis was money hungry. The more famous Purvis became, the more that rumor trailed behind him. Hoover seemed to confirm the rumors when, in his own book, he lied, claiming that Purvis had not resigned but had instead been fired. Then Hoover swamped the public with his official version of the Dillinger story. *G-Men,* a radio series that began in the summer of 1935, cut both Purvis and the Woman in Red out entirely. Instead, the faceless technicians of the Bureau's crime lab identified Dillinger through his fingerprints; Cowley led the battle with the aid of a newly invented agent named Nellis, who lit the all-important cigar. While Purvis appeared on cereal boxes, Hoover spoke to young people in *G-Men* comic strips, and his photograph began showing up on the society pages.

THE MAN WHO INVENTED GOSSIP

"GOOD EVENING, MR. AND MRS. AMERICA"

"Did you know?" "Have you heard?" People have always loved learning hot secrets and juicy rumors about neighbors, rivals, and especially the great and famous. Up until the 1920s, gossip was shared in person, friend to friend. Today, every trip to the supermarket can tell you which celebrity is "showing" or snuck out for a wild party with an ex-girlfriend. Sites like TMZ keep you up to the tweeting second on the so-called private lives of movie stars, music stars, and people who are stars simply because their lives are constantly filmed and photographed. We owe this whole buzzing world of seamy secrets—as addictive as popcorn—to one man: Walter Winchell.

When Winchell began writing for newspapers in the 1920s, the press treated the private world as off-limits. You could not say that a woman was pregnant, could not report on marital infidelity unless that came out in a court case. You could not mention a politician's affairs, no matter how often he appeared in public with a favored mistress. Winchell changed the rules. He wrote in a new style: short sentences . . . separated by ellipses . . . punchy and telegraphic.

He invented words that almost said what you couldn't say, as if he were speaking in whisper, confiding a secret just to

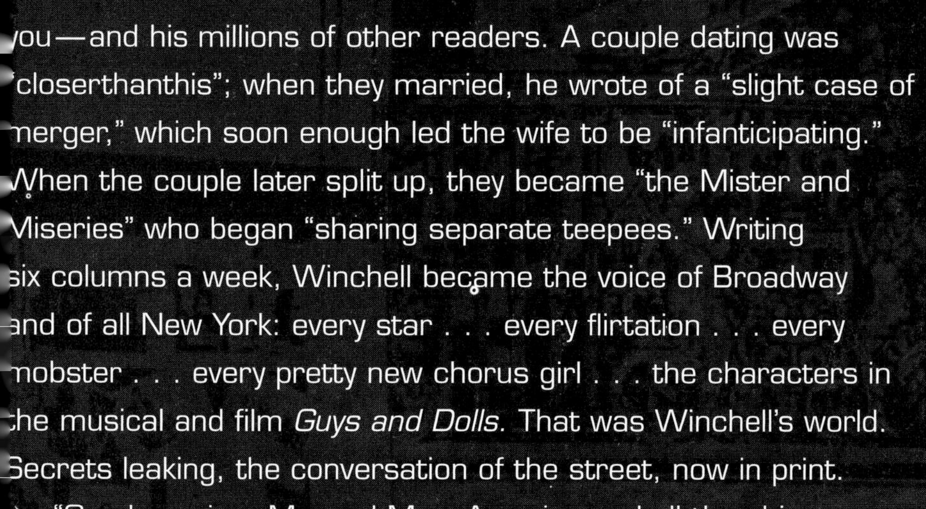

you—and his millions of other readers. A couple dating was "closerthanthis"; when they married, he wrote of a "slight case of merger," which soon enough led the wife to be "infanticipating." When the couple later split up, they became "the Mister and Miseries" who began "sharing separate teepees." Writing six columns a week, Winchell became the voice of Broadway and of all New York: every star . . . every flirtation . . . every mobster . . . every pretty new chorus girl . . . the characters in the musical and film *Guys and Dolls.* That was Winchell's world. Secrets leaking, the conversation of the street, now in print.

"Good evening, Mr. and Mrs. America and all the ships at sea." By 1930 Winchell had his own radio show, which he began with that call to the nation. He was speaking directly to all Americans, talking about politics, exposing Nazi spies and sympathizers. Hoover knew secrets but always wanted to know more. He put Winchell on a list of favored reporters who got the earliest and best stories of Bureau exploits. Hoover assigned an agent to listen to every Winchell broadcast to gather more secrets. It was a perfect circle: Winchell lavished praise on Hoover, Hoover made sure Winchell knew more than his rivals, and America listened in.

THE CLUB

If you wanted to be seen in the 1930s, there was just one place to go: the Stork Club at 3 East Fifty-third Street, just off Fifth Avenue, in New York City. You were let into the club only if its owner, the ex-bootlegger Sherman Billingsley, wanted you there. You had to be rich, well known in society, a famous artist, an equally famous criminal, a favored reporter, or a special friend.

The Stork was all about being special. Not only did you have to get past the doorman to be allowed in, but there was a separate space, the Cub Room, for the real elite. Table 50 in the inner sanctum was reserved for Walter Winchell, who held court there, eating food specially prepared to his liking and gathering the nation's secrets. Billingsley made sure that every chosen patron felt at home: he "found out his favorite drink, his favorite cigar . . . his friends, his relatives, everything about everybody." While only the favored few (which meant no blacks and few Jews) could actually get into the club, Winchell and the news photographers kept the eyes of the waiting public trained on the glamour and celebrity buzz that filled the Stork every night. As Hoover became more famous, he took weekend trips up from Washington to New York, where he was guaranteed his own seat in the inner room. In the popping of flashbulbs and the buzz of the gossip columns, the whole nation could see its top cop, its strong man, smiling alongside millionaires and movie stars.

Indeed, the final showdown between Hoover and Purvis took place at the movies. Hollywood liked Purvis, but Hoover made sure that it *loved* the Bureau. In the early 1930s, the film industry was in trouble with critics who felt that movies were too racy and celebrated the wrong kinds of heroes. Hollywood agreed to police itself but still wanted as much shoot-'em-up action as it could get. Hoover provided the perfect answer: as he fed stories directly from the Bureau's files to Hollywood, he offered heroism,

Hoover celebrating New Year's Eve 1935 at the Stork Club, seated with Tolson. Nightclubs were places for adults to have fun—with music, dancing, and silly hats—and Hoover's participation increased his celebrity.

crime-does-not-pay messages, and the crackle of gunfire. "See Uncle Sam draw his guns to halt the march of crime," the movie ads screamed.

The media is fickle. It will blaze the image of the latest hero across the sky, then ignore him completely. For a moment Melvin Purvis was the great detective every American knew. And then he was gone: not the hero, not the pitchman, not on cereal boxes, not in the Bureau, not even able to find work

SCOOP!
THE FIRST AUTHENTIC (FACTUAL NOT FICTION) PICTURES
OF HOOVER, HIMSELF, AND
HIS G-MEN, BEHIND THE
SCENES AND IN ACTION!
THE New UNIVERSAL presents
JOHN EDGAR HOOVER
DIRECTOR
Federal Bureau of Investigation
United States Department of Justice
Washington, D. C.
October 30, 1936
It is indeed gratifying that the Universal Pictures Corporation is producing the short feature picture entitled "You Can't Get Away With It," depicting the first factual scenes of the activities of the Federal Bureau of Investigation, Department of Justice, in its warfare against organized crime throughout the United States.
The picture is made up of interesting, dramatic, and authentic facts, and I feel that it will serve a most useful purpose in impressing upon millions of minds -- especially those of the youth of the country -- the fact that a life of crime is a sordid one. Also, I believe the production will serve to further encourage cooperation between the general public and the members of the law enforcement profession, which is so necessary if organized crime in the United States is to be curbed.
J. Edgar Hoover
John Edgar Hoover,
Director.
PRESENTED WITH THE PERMISSION OF
HON. HOMER S. CUMMINGS
ATTORNEY GENERAL OF THE U.S.
AND WITH THE COOPERATION OF
J. EDGAR HOOVER
DIRECTOR
FEDERAL BUREAU of INVESTIGATION
OF THE
DEPARTMENT of JUSTICE
WANTED
WANTED
JOHN HERBERT DILLINGER
$10,000.00
$5,000.00
"YOU CAN'T GET AWAY WITH IT!"
NARRATED by
LOWELL THOMAS
Produced by
CHARLES E. FORD
A UNIVERSAL PICTURE
SEE
THE NERVE CENTRE OF THE F. B. I.—THE KIDNAP SWITCHBOARD!—LEARN THE INTIMATE SECRETS OF GANGDOM!—HOW "G" MEN TRAIN FOR WAR AGAINST CRIME!—THE SCIENTIFIC CRIME-BUSTING LABORATORY!—SECRETS OF THE FINGERPRINT BUREAU!—THE "ARSENALS" CAPTURED WITH OUTLAWS!—LEARN THE INSIDE STORY OF HOW DILLINGER, KARPIS, NELSON, THE BAILEYS AND OTHERS WERE CAPTURED!—SEE THE WAR MAP OF THE "G" MEN!—THE AMAZING "MONIKER" FILE OF GANGSTER MOLLS!—THE MURDEROUS HISTORY OF GANGSTER GUNS!—DEADLY MARKSMANSHIP OF THE "G" MEN!—HOW WASHED OUT BLOOD-STAINS ARE MADE VISIBLE AGAIN!—CRIMINALS CAUGHT THROUGH MARKINGS ON BULLETS!—SMUDGE TURNED INTO DEADLY CLUES!—THE CRACKING OF FAMOUS KIDNAPING CASES!—THE REAL "G" MEN ON THE SCREEN FOR THE FIRST TIME!

providing security for businesses. Each time he applied for a new job, Hoover got there first with private warnings that Purvis was not reliable. The director's revenge was endless and relentless. In 1960, Purvis took out his Bureau revolver, walked off alone, and killed himself.

Hoover's system was indeed more powerful than any individual; the arms of the Bureau could crush even the most popular hero in America. He won the war of images, erasing the "mincing step" story by appearing on movie billboards with guns blazing, ending the popular reign of the Public Enemy by gunning down Dillinger, and eclipsing the star of his lawman rival.

Everywhere you looked, there was Hoover, playing the part of the G-man hero. "You Can't Get Away with It!" announced one film based on real cases. And that is the message he was eager to convey. The Federal Bureau of Investigation, or FBI, as the Bureau was renamed in 1935, was the thin but strong skeleton of vigilance and science that stood behind good old-fashioned American life—always there, always watching, always ready. Hoover himself was a media star; photographers snapped shots of him enjoying baseball games and rooting at horse races; chatting at the Stork Club; showing off shotguns to film stars, spelling-bee winners, and Boy Scout troops at the FBI shooting gallery. He and Clyde Tolson pranced about in their identical suits—so well dressed and full of high-spirited fun that they could laugh at what people might make of them. But the next challenge Hoover faced was more daunting than *Collier's*, Dillinger, and Purvis combined: popular Communism.

Opposite: The poster says it all—the film sells Hoover, just as Hoover's approval allows the movie studio to fill the screen with nonstop action.

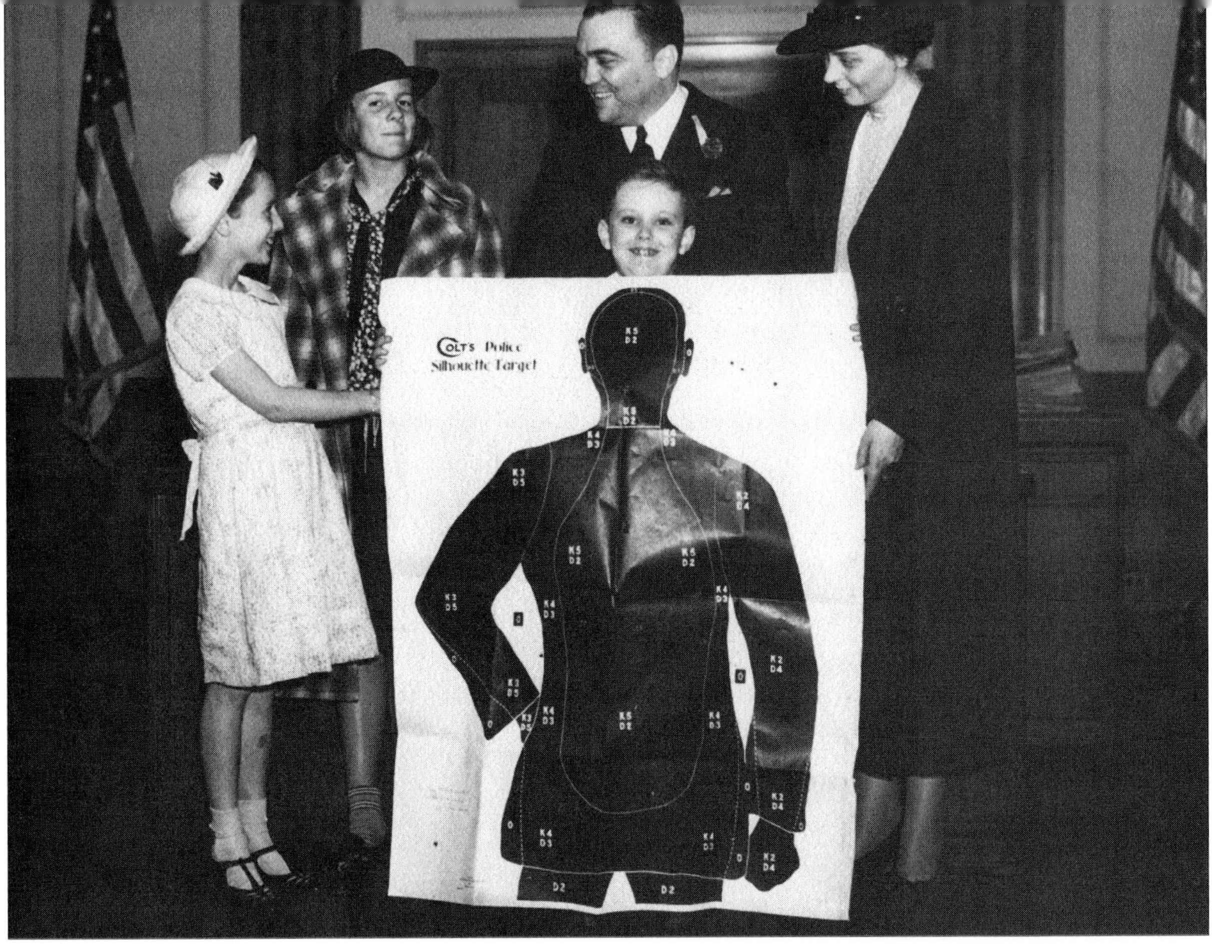

Above: Young people enjoyed visiting headquarters and having their picture taken with Hoover, and every local paper carried the story.

Right: Hoover takes a group of Hollywood actors to the FBI rifle range. His own shooting pose is as staged as theirs; he made only two arrests in the field, both carefully set up so that he could arrive to bring in the criminal to the pop of flashbulbs.

Left: Hoover and Tolson in close conversation with Walter Winchell. Winchell made sure the public kept reading and hearing about Hoover's triumphs.

Below: Shirley Temple was just one of an endless parade of movie stars photographed with Hoover. The publicity was as good for the actors, who wanted to be seen as good citizens, as it was for Hoover, who was selling the power and prestige of his organization.

8 THE CRISIS OF CAPITALISM: THE THIRD SECRET

BASEBALL IN MOSCOW

The breadlines and shattered dreams of the Great Depression gave the Communist Party its golden opportunity to win over Americans and start the revolution. Proof of Marx's theories shone in every headline about collapsing banks, skyrocketing unemployment, and desperate, angry men. Where capitalists seemed at best ineffectual and at worst heartless, Communism offered an answer. Not only that but the Communists had a nation, Russia, where the future was on display for all to see. As Joseph Freeman, an American Communist put it, "At the very moment when our own country, to the surprise of all except the Marxists, was sliding into a social-economic abyss, the new social-economic system of the Russian workers and peasants showed striking gains."

The people in front of the billboard in this photo are lining up for bread after a flood in Louisville, Kentucky. The famous photo was taken in 1937 by Margaret Bourke-White and speaks volumes about the contrast between the all-white, prosperous, image of America and the harsh realities of the time.

In 1931, for the first and only time in American history, more people were leaving the country than arriving at its shores. Over one hundred thousand of those Americans seeking better opportunities applied to move to Russia in the first eight months of the year alone. Just as Marx had predicted, workers were fleeing from the crisis of capitalism and flocking to the land where the future was being built by their own hands.

When Americans arrived in Moscow with their families, they were full of optimism. Their kids went to a special Anglo-American school that was stocked with books by authors they knew and liked, such as Jack London, Mark Twain, and Charles Dickens. Their slightly older brothers formed baseball teams, which were so popular that Russians began to take up the sport.

In 1933, for example, thirteen-year-old Lucy Abolin moved from Boston to Moscow, where her father took a job as a metalworker. She quickly became a star at the Anglo-American school. Her brothers, Arthur and Carl, played for the Moscow Foreign Workers baseball team. The Abolins were a poster family for the appeal of being Americans in the Workers' Paradise.

HOOVER'S THIRD SECRET

Back in America, the Communists were famously well organized and fearless, which made them ideal union organizers. In the 1930s, they spread out to help workers fight for their rights. Even if a factory hand did not care about Marx or Lenin, he was glad to have a strong, effective voice on his side, arguing for better wages or shorter hours. Communists pushed to organize automobile plants, waterfront docks, and Mexican-American and Asian-American farmworkers. Wherever there were Americans in need, Americans ignored, neglected, or oppressed, the Communists sought them out and offered a helping hand.

In addition to its direct attacks on injustice, the Communist Party backed numerous organizations devoted to good causes: foster parents for children caught up in foreign wars, the American Youth Congress, the Abolish Peonage Committee to fight for the rights of southern farmworkers. To well-meaning citizens, these groups provided a way to help others, and the fact that the Party was somehow involved with them hardly mattered.

The strong, active organizers combined with the seeming death throes of capitalism brought newcomers to the Party. Membership

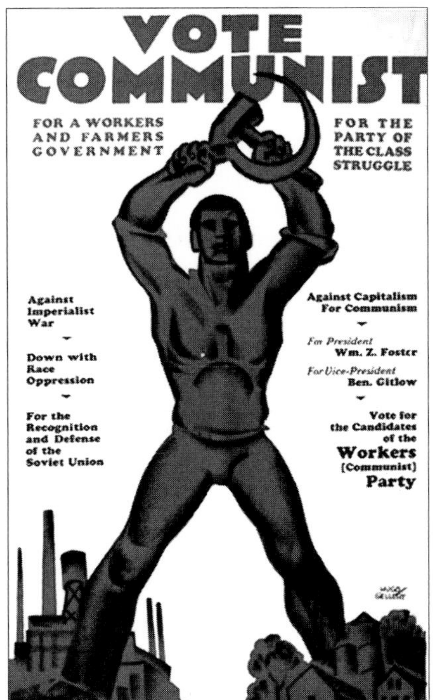

This poster for the American Communist Party was designed by Hugo Gellert, whose images of muscular workers influenced the creators of Superman. Ben Gitlow, named here as a vice-presidential candidate, worked with John Reed on radical papers and was arrested during the November 7, 1919, raid Hoover organized.

quadrupled from around ten thousand in the mid-1920s to forty thousand in 1936, then doubled to eighty-two thousand in 1938. How could the Party grow further? Back in 1920, John Reed had urged the Second Congress of International Communism to reach out to American blacks, "an enslaved and oppressed people." A decade later, Moscow told American Communists to follow that lead. The Communist Party ticket in the 1932 presidential election featured James W. Ford as its vice-presidential candidate — the first American of African descent to be nominated for national office. Ford had been head of the Harlem branch of the Party. Benjamin Davis, his successor, went on to be elected to New York's City Council.

Earl Browder and James W. Ford first ran together in 1932, when they received just over 100,000 votes — not close to the millions needed to win, but more than twice the 48,000 votes the Party had earned in 1928.

Hoover's deepest belief was that Communists were calculating liars. He was certain that all the "front" groups they created, which claimed to help workers, farmers, orphaned children, were just props in their plot to destroy the America he knew and loved. As he saw it, the Party was using apparently good causes to suck people in, brainwash them, and turn them into its robotic agents. People who joined such groups but never actually became Communists were, to him, "fellow travelers" — dupes who helped the Party achieve its ends.

Was Hoover right? Were the Communists just using foolish or mushy-brained liberals who refused to recognize the Party's cynical calculations? Or were the Communists right? Were their clear thinking and tight organizational structure a lifeline to helpless people in a time of crisis? One test case was the black community, which leads to what may have been Hoover's third secret.

Hoover mistrusted everything the Communists did, but there was something deeper, more sinister, more personal in his reactions to any effort to improve the lives of black people. He viewed black Americans as a kind of sleeping beast that could be ignited into blind, destructive fury. Even before the Depression, he had sent his agents out to bring down the black nationalist leader Marcus Garvey. Hoover saw Garvey as a potential "Negro Moses"—a kind of Antichrist who would dazzle black people and mislead them into attacking whites. He managed to have Garvey imprisoned and then deported. "The colored people," he said as late as 1965, "are quite ignorant, mostly uneducated, and I doubt if they would seek an education if they had the opportunity."

Why did Hoover react so strongly to the issue of black rights? He was hardly alone in his views, and it may be that his upbringing in segregated Washington explains enough. Yet rumors, family legends, and intriguing-but-inconclusive genealogical records suggest that Hoover's family was partially African American but "passing" as white. Indeed, when you browse through endless files of Hoover photographs, he comes across as a racial chameleon—sometimes very dark, sometimes much lighter; in the rare cases when he was photographed in left profile, he distinctly resembles fair-skinned African Americans such as Congressman Adam Clayton Powell Jr. This is a mystery that only a dedicated researcher armed with DNA samples and assisted by Hoover family relatives can fully resolve. And even if there were a secret African-American root in his family tree, we have no evidence that he was aware of it.

The one thing we can say about Hoover's possible secrets—the tensions in his childhood home, the question of his sexuality, and the rumors about his mixed ancestry—is that something was so close to boiling over inside him that he needed to maintain total control. Hoover had no tolerance for ideas or emotions that threatened his world. All too often he assumed that anyone seeking to improve the lot of American blacks was a Communist. A master of deceit himself, he was keenly aware of the plots and deceptions his enemies might well be hatching.

Opposite: At a glance, this is yet another bland publicity shot with visitors. But look at Hoover's hands clutching the tabletop, perhaps a sign of strain. The sapphire ring was a present from his mother that he wore throughout his life.

PHOTO DOSSIER:
Those who think they know what Hoover looked like are most often recalling images of him from the very end of his life, when he was ill and almost pasty white. These images of a younger Hoover allow for questions about his family's racial history.

Above: Out in the sunshine, a very dark Hoover

Right: Hoover ten years later, looking lighter but what might now be called Hispanic

Opposite: Greeting an African-American father and son and standing in profile, which highlights his wavy hair, Hoover looks distinctly African American. Compare this image to photos of prominent African Americans of the time such as Walter White, who led the NAACP from the 1930s until the mid-1950s, or Harlem congressman Adam Clayton Powell Jr., and it would be easy to think of Hoover as the product of a racially mixed heritage.

THE TEST CASE: SCOTTSBORO, ALABAMA, 1931

A black male could not be in worse trouble than to be accused of raping a white woman in Alabama. Accusation almost always led to conviction, and 100 percent of blacks found guilty of that crime, no matter the circumstances, were executed. So when two white Alabama women accused nine young black males—the youngest was twelve, the oldest twenty-one—of brutal and repeated gang rape, their fates seemed to be sealed. The judge's biggest challenge was keeping the accused away from a lynch mob in Scottsboro, where they were being held, so that they would live long enough to be tried. The local defense lawyers the judge managed to scrounge up were totally ineffective; one of them appeared to be so drunk on the first day of the trial that he stumbled around the courthouse. The nine were instantly convicted and sentenced to be executed. And that is where the Communists stepped in.

Anyone who reads about the case today will immediately see that the two women (one of whom was married and the other a teenager) invented the whole story to cover up their own affairs with other men. One actually admitted that soon enough. But getting a court to agree required challenging the entire Alabama system of justice. The Communist Party hired Samuel Leibowitz, one of the very best lawyers in the country, to take on the apparently hopeless case. In trial after retrial, appeal after appeal, the case against the nine fell apart, yet they remained in jail, often in solitary confinement or on death row. It was not until 1950 that all the accused were safe: released, paroled, or—in one case—escaped from prison and protected by the order of the governor of another state.

As the years went by, the Scottsboro trials split the black community. Moderate leaders tried desperately to wrest the case from the Communist Party. But many people, black and white, saw the Party as strong, determined, and helpful. Every Party rally or demonstration aimed to bring together everyone who cared about racism, poverty, and social justice.

The great novelist Richard Wright had grown up poor and black in the South, and left high school to work. But he had such a hunger to learn that

The

SCOTTSBORO BOYS MUST NOT DIE!

MASS SCOTTSBORO DEFENSE MEETING

At St. Mark's M. E. Church

137th Street and St. Nicholas Avenue

Friday Eve., April 14th, 8 P. M.

Protest the infamous death verdict rendered by an all-white jury at Decatur, Alabama against HAYWOOD PATTERSON

The Meeting will be addressed by:

Mrs. JANIE PATTERSON, mother of Haywood Patterson, victim of the lynch verdict; SAMUEL LEIBOWITZ, chief counsel for the defense; JOSEPH BRODSKY, defense counsel; WILLIAM PATTERSON, National Secretary of the I. L. D.; RICHARD B. MOORE; Dr. LORENZO KING; WM. KELLEY of the Amsterdam News; and others.

THUNDER YOUR INDIGNATION AGAINST THE JUDICIAL MURDER OF INNOCENT NEGRO CHILDREN!

COME TO THE MASS PROTEST MEETING

AT ST. MARK'S M. E. CHURCH

137th Street and St. Nicholas Avenue

FRIDAY EVENING, APRIL 14th, 8 P. M.

Emergency Scctt sboro Defense Committee

119 West 135th Street, New York City

Rallies such as the one promoted in this poster showed the Communist Party in the best light—leading the way to protect innocent lives from racist injustice.

he educated himself and sensed that he wanted to write. In Chicago he met a group of Communists—the first white people who ever seemed to take him seriously. The Communists convinced him that only they understood the "overwhelming drama of moral struggle" that was taking place around the world. Wright joined the Party.

Scottsboro, it might seem, proved that the Party was right and Hoover was wrong. He was blinded by his prejudices, while the radical revolutionaries saw through the lies of American history. But that is not the end of the story. The Communists were as inhuman and calculating as Hoover claimed—and the proof of that lay in the arts.

"YOU ARE PIONEERS OR YOU ARE NOTHING"

The Communist Party insisted that the Depression proved that its understanding of world events was correct. Marx, and thus Marxists, knew the truth of the past, present, and future. But since that was so, the Party claimed it had the right to dictate exactly what every writer and actor, poet and painter, should create. Mike Gold, a good American Communist, explained that all older forms of fiction, poetry, drama, and music were a product of the diseased, dying capitalist world that "isolated each artist as in a solitary cell, there to brood and suffer silently and go mad." Now that capitalism was collapsing, artists had a new mission: to portray "the revolution . . . the strike, boycott, mass-meeting." The truth of the world was the clash of classes, and everyone needed to line up with the workers or be swept aside.

Artists who listened to Gold stopped writing about their personal feelings or their imaginative fantasies. Instead, they dutifully crafted stories and plays designed to spur the audience to strike, to act, to join the Party. Anyone who resisted, who felt that artists needed to follow their own inner light, was condemned as a traitor. *The New Masses,* the American Communists' monthly magazine, screamed out the only two possible futures for artists: "You are either pioneers and builders of civilization, or you are nothing. You will either aid in moulding history, or history will mould you." Those who failed to see the light and join in the Communist revolution faced a terrible fate: "You will be indescribably crushed and maimed in the process. And the end will be total destruction."

Art was no longer a personal expression; it was a weapon in the revolutionary cause. That meant artists needed to bend to the will of the Party.

This 1933 issue of the New Masses *is a cross section of the American Communist Party at the time: it defended the Scottsboro boys and raised the alarm over the Nazis when too many others did not notice or did not care, but it also insisted that writers devote their art to the cause of class revolution.*

Ever since the mid-nineteenth century, when Communists and other advocates for workers gathered to demand that the work day be limited to eight hours—rather than ten or twelve—May 1, or May Day, has been the occasion for rallies. In New York City, where this photo was taken, the rallies were often held in Union Square—which took its name from the nearby union offices.

While the Communists were eager to make Richard Wright a member of the Party, they were suspicious of him. They didn't like his clean shirts and tasteful tie, his well-shined shoes. He seemed too much of a bookish intellectual, not the hearty black laborer the Party wanted. And when he refused to obey Party commands about where and how to teach, he was kicked out.

One day in May, Wright went to a Party rally in Chicago, and an old friend invited him to march with the Communists. As he began to walk, a voice barked, "Get out of our ranks!" "I-It's May Day and I want to march," he protested. "Get out." Soon, as Wright wrote, "hands lifted me bodily from the sidewalk. I felt myself being pitched headlong through the air. . . . The rows of white and black Communists were looking at me with cold eyes of nonrecognition. . . . Suddenly, the vast ranks of the Communist Party began to move. Scarlet banners with the hammer and sickle emblem of world revolution were lifted, and they fluttered in the May breeze. . . . A long line of set-faced men and women, white and black, flowed past me."

Wright saw what the marching masses could not: "they're blind." The ranks of Party members moved in lockstep like a grim, sightless machine. He left the Party and went on to write such pathbreaking novels as *Native Son* and *Black Boy.*

In the drama of the global depression, people were constantly pushed to choose a side — to see one nation, one party, as all good (and thus to ignore its failings) and another as entirely evil (and thus to dismiss any cause it supported). For the moment many believed that the Communists and their supporters had the upper hand. They waved the flag of their concern for the masses, their defense of the Scottsboro Nine, their beautiful Soviet Union. Hoover continued to gather evidence of Communist influences on liberal causes. But — ever the smart politician — he made sure no one knew exactly how his agents got their information. He was collecting names to use when the time was ripe. For now, he focused on becoming indispensable to the incoming president, Franklin Roosevelt. He succeeded all too well.

PART THREE

THE STORY: In 1933, the United States recognized the Communist government of the Soviet Union, a move that allowed the Soviets to establish embassies in America. In exchange, the Soviets promised to pay debts that had been on the books since before the Russian Revolution, to guarantee freedom of religion for Americans visiting Russia, and not to attempt to spread Communism in America. All the promises were lies.

THE FACTS: The Soviets immediately used their diplomatic passports and embassies to spy, infiltrate, and attempt to subvert the United States. It took a man with his ear to the ground, listening for whispers, watching for shadows, to sense the growing network of spies.

The Turning Point: Subversive Activities

Background photograph: Hoover standing directly behind President Franklin Delano Roosevelt on July 26, 1933. The kidnapping of an Oklahoma City businessman was in the headlines, but by September, Hoover's men had captured the criminals, one of whom was said to have yelled, "Don't shoot, G-Men" — giving the lawmen their nickname.

Standing in front of a monumental portrait of George Washington, American Nazis show their colors, claiming that they are true Americans. This photo was taken at a large American Nazi party rally in New York City in 1939.

THE SECRET ASSIGNMENT

Summer 1936: J. Edgar Hoover was wanted on the phone: Major General Smedley Butler was on the line. Butler was a true hero who had twice earned the Congressional Medal of Honor, then retired after being the head of the marines. If he was calling, it must be important. He was contacting Hoover to report that extreme right-wing Americans had approached him to head up a private army and invade Mexico. This was the second time recruiters had come to the much-honored soldier. Two years earlier, some of the richest men in the country—key stockholders in such companies as General Motors, DuPont, and U.S. Steel—had put together a fund to orchestrate a coup to overthrow President Roosevelt. Butler was beloved by his men, so the wealthy cabal was certain he was the one leader who could march into Washington and change the government. Butler turned down the first overture in 1934 and had just said no again. He was calling to pass along the story of the plot to Hoover.

After taking down the information, Hoover made sure the president was informed. The more danger and unrest there was in the country, the bigger the job for the FBI.

In the early 1930s, it really did seem possible that a coup could take place in the United States. Some 25 percent of Americans who wanted to work could not find jobs, leaving millions of angry, unemployed people. Americans were losing faith in their government, and when you no longer trust elected officials, you begin to take alternatives—even violent ones—seriously. In 1934 alone, nearly one and a half million workers participated in some 1,800 strikes. What if men in steel mills, ports, and power stations walked off the job? Couldn't they cripple the nation and open the way to a rebellion led by a strong leader? After all, exactly those kinds of uprisings were already taking place in Europe.

Groups with names like the Silver Shirts and the German-American Bund marched to show that they supported the Nazis in Germany and wanted a similar government in America. A Texas oil baron bankrolled another fringe organization that railed against taxes, rights for blacks, and Roosevelt's "Jew Deal," which it claimed was part of an international plot

hatched by wealthy bankers. And then there were the Communists. In 1933, when the Russians were allowed to open embassies in America, it became all too easy for them to look for allies and to begin spying for the homeland. As one agent later recalled, "If you wore a sign saying 'I Am a Spy,' you might still not get arrested."

By the end of the summer of 1936, FDR had heard enough. Between Hoover's memo about the Butler plot and other tips about Soviet spying, he knew there was real danger brewing. On August 24, he called Hoover in to figure out how to guard against what Hoover would later term "subversive activities in the United States." Whose job was that? The Secret Service kept its ear to the ground for plots, but its only responsibility was to protect the president himself, not the nation. What about the FBI? The Bureau had absolutely no authority to deal with the kind of threat that concerned the president. But Hoover had an idea.

Hoover knew how to find loopholes in rules and regulations the way a dog sniffs out a hidden bone. Way back in 1916, a budget bill had instructed the Bureau to investigate "any matters referred to it by the Department of State." Any matters. So if the secretary of state were to tell the FBI to go after "subversives"—whatever that meant and whoever they were—the Bureau would simply be doing what Congress had long ago told it to do. FDR liked the idea but took a night to think it over. The next day, Roosevelt called a secret meeting. As Hoover recalled, there, in private, FDR said that he wanted this to "be handled quite confidentially and that the President, Secretary of State, and I should be the ones aware of this request."

That secret conversation was the moment when Hoover's life story changed American history. He was given real authority to protect the nation, which he slowly but surely transformed into the right to play by his own rules, even if that totally undermined the laws and principles of the democracy he was protecting.

Opposite: During the 1939 Nazi rally in New York, a Jewish man who rushed the stage was severely beaten. The attack was captured by photographer Alfred Eisenstaedt, and his photos of it were published in Life *magazine. Nazism was alive and dangerous in America.*

On May 18, 1934, President Roosevelt signed a package of anti-crime legislation that extended the powers and responsibilities of Hoover's bureau. The more significant and dangerous extension of the FBI took place in a private meeting two years later. Hoover was the only one to ever describe that discussion, so we have only his word for the mandate given to him by the president.

FDR's request was the opening Hoover had been waiting for since the last Palmer raid sixteen years earlier. And it came exactly in the way he wanted it: a secret deal, never to be revealed to Congress, not subject to any review except by the three men in the room and Hoover's direct boss, the attorney general. This was Hoover, the brilliant bureaucrat, making absolutely sure that a powerful person above him in the Washington hierarchy gave him orders, a mandate that he would then use to vastly expand his own power. In fact, by 1938, he confidently stated to the president that the FBI's mission was "broad enough to cover any expansion" of secret "intelligence and counter-espionage work." "Any expansion." In the cold light of history, those two words are terrifying. Indeed, the agreement the president and the director were determined to keep secret was the foundation of the FBI's intricately defended empire of surveillance and subversion for the next forty years.

Every nation has its secrets and its guardians; after all, countries do face real enemies. But when the person charged with exposing and capturing those spies and traitors is allowed to operate in the dark, out of sight, the country begins to rot from within. That is Hoover's tragedy: he was able to live out his lifetime dream, the job of safeguarding America his own way, by his own rules. But, as we now know, step by step, year by year, the dream became ever more of a nightmare for free-thinking Americans.

To be fair, Hoover never acted entirely alone. He always made sure he had some sort of clearance from his immediate superior, the attorney general, and his ultimate boss, the president. In fact, it was in working to curry favor with FDR and to undermine the president's political enemies that Hoover really began to use his toolbox of controversial activities. Hoover insisted that his agents follow the letter of the law — or at least not explicitly break the law. However, as an astute lawyer and lifetime Washington insider, he knew exactly how to get around these regulations.

By 1939, Europe was at war. Would America join in? Polls showed that the voting public was strongly against doing so. But FDR recognized the danger posed by Nazi Germany and Japan, as well as the dire threats to England, America's closest ally. He needed to walk a careful political tightrope to lend support to the heroes fighting against the Nazis without alarming voters. His job was all the more difficult because those determined to keep America out of the growing conflict found a popular spokesman in Charles Lindbergh and a voice in the growing America First Committee (AFC). FDR was certain that Lindbergh was a Nazi, which was a perfect opening for Hoover. The more dirt Hoover could gather about Lindbergh and America First—legally or illegally—the happier FDR would be.

Charles Lindbergh (middle figure, in dark jacket) addresses an America First rally in Madison Square Garden in 1941. (The man with his hand raised is Senator Burton K. Wheeler.)

Wiretapping—listening in on private phone conversations—was illegal. Congress had said so in 1934, and the Supreme Court agreed. But neither FDR nor Hoover accepted that. In 1940, the president secretly ruled that wiretaps could be used in special cases involving national defense, so long as the attorney general personally approved each one. Hoover was to keep a log of authorized taps, which the attorney general could review at any time. But this system of checks did not reckon with Hoover's gift for evading rules and hiding in plain sight. When he wanted to tap a line but did not have approval, he omitted it from the logbook. Instead, the record was kept in the secret card files of his top assistants, then destroyed after six months. FDR may or may not have guessed that Hoover was making up his own rules. But so long as the result was information that could embarrass or undermine those who opposed his policies in Europe, he did not mind. On June 14, 1940, he sent Hoover a note expressing his deep "appreciation" "for the many interesting and valuable reports that you have made to me."

J. Edgar Hoover truly understood the power of filing. Every action undertaken by FBI agents was described, recorded, and explained. Hoover needed to know, and have a defense for, absolutely everything that went on in his agency. But the fact that his eyes were everywhere did not mean the outside world was permitted the same sight.

As far back as the 1920s, Hoover had set up a raft of discrete filing systems so that everything he needed to know would flow to him but would be hidden from outsiders. According to New York congressman Emanuel Celler, Hoover had a file "on every member of Congress and every member of the Senate." Whenever a senator drank too much and had a brush with the law, whenever a representative checked into a hotel room with a woman who wasn't his wife, whenever rumors swirled about a powerful man who was attracted to men, Hoover found out and noted the details on a file card. Reports like this were called Summary Memoranda and were kept in sealed envelopes. Since they were not part of the regular FBI record system, Hoover could truthfully say that the Bureau kept no files on politicians. He also kept track of other sexual material—for example, pornographic books, films, and records. These were placed in an Obscene File, which was kept in Hoover's office and also not listed in the public files.

FBI agents mastered the art of the "black-bag job," which meant breaking into the office of a person or organization to plant a microphone or to rifle through notebooks, diaries, and calendars. These undercover actions violated the Fourth Amendment to the Constitution, which protects against "unreasonable searches." As a result, they were recorded in a file titled Do Not File. That way, if an inquisitive outsider asked for damaging files, they would not exist. How could investigators ask for something they had no way of knowing about? Some illegal acts were described in files that were destroyed every six months, but an "executive summary" of the now-missing files was kept separately, in a Confidential File. There was even a third level of file: the Personal and Confidential, files that Hoover's loyal secretary hurried to shred just after he died.

Hoover gathered secrets the way Gollum in *The Lord of the Rings* pursues the ring—they were his "precious." In time his men would add new methods of illegal surveillance, such as planting listening devices in private rooms and intercepting telegrams or steaming open letters to read people's correspondence.

Only Hoover and his most trusted men knew what the many secret reports actually contained—which set up yet another layer of deception. None of their snooping, legal or illegal, turned up proof that the Nazis were behind the America First Committee. In fact, agents discovered that the committee was trying to steer clear of extremists and had no foreign backing. As obnoxious as the beliefs and arguments of the AFC were to those eager to confront Hitler, it was a political pressure group legally exercising its right to speak. Hoover hid those reports and instead continued to feed the president bits of negative information about his political enemies. Not only did the FBI gather information illegally; it also lied about what it discovered. Hoover's goal, and thus that of his extremely loyal lieutenants, was to please the president while extending the Bureau's secret power. As 1941 neared its end and war loomed, the FBI was like a tree: its leaves turned to the warm sun of presidential approval, its roots extending ever farther into the underground soil.

From 1936 on into the war years, danger performed its magic. Because America faced such real threats, Hoover gained vastly more power. He was visible as an image of the Protector of the Law, yet invisibly, behind the scenes, he could bend, break, or ignore the law. That combination of patriotic propaganda and covert abuse is extremely dangerous. Hoover figured out how to violate the rights of anyone he chose while simultaneously recording everything and hiding anything that could endanger him. By marrying this carefully plotted structure of lawbreaking and deceit with his systematic policy of collecting Washington secrets, Hoover gained a stranglehold on the country. In the name of the law, he was outside the law. And that was only one layer of his dark power.

JUNE FILES

This memo, now available on the FBI website, details how files called "June," which mentioned "confidential investigative techniques," were to be taken out of the regular filing system and housed only in abstracts. The memo cautions that access to the abstracts must be carefully controlled, since they are "most revealing."

JUNE

SECURITY OF CRIMINAL INTELLIGENCE INFORMATION

b6
b7C

INSPECTOR [redacted]

During course of the inspection inquiry was made into the security afforded criminal intelligence information. It was discovered that no case files were designated for restricted handling or kept on file in the Special File Room apart from other Bureau files. In the Inspector's opinion some of these cases are analogous to double agent cases in the security field and the files should be afforded the same degree of protection. Of primary concern here are those files which contain information so revealing such that because of its very nature, if disclosed serious damage would result to Bureau's over-all program in the criminal intelligence field. Examples of such files are those on La Cosa Nostra, leaders of La Cosa Nostra and Top Echelon Criminal Informants.

b2
b6
b7C

Communications bearing code word "JUNE" which relate to microphone surveillances and other highly confidential investigative techniques are not placed in the case files to which they relate but are correctly maintained in the Special File Room and given restricted handling. However, this precaution is negated by the fact that abstracts summarizing these communications are filed along with and maintained in same manner as all other abstracts in the case. These abstracts are most revealing as they contain such statements as the following: "Mike was installed with trespass"; "All Bureau [redacted] equipment in connection with misur installation at [redacted] Beverly Hills, Calif., removed 9/11/62"; [redacted] discontinued this date. Microphone and attending wires removed."

OBSERVATIONS:

A. In the event a decision is made to maintain certain selected files in Special File Room, this precaution would be circumvented if the abstracts were too detailed. In these cases the field would have to be instructed to not include sensitive criminal intelligence information in abstracts. As an additional security measure Files and Communications Division might place a regulation in effect whereby the abstracts relating to these cases could not be charged out without approval of appropriate Assistant Director or Section Chief.

ALL INFORMATION CONTAINED
HEREIN IS UNCLASSIFIED
DATE 07-16-2008

SPECIAL INVESTIGATIVE DIVISION INSPECTION
9/24/64
ACM:wmj

ENCLOSURE

Orig-220

Hoover kept refining the public-relations formula he had crafted in the Gangster Era: whispering campaigns to undermine rivals combined with ever more books, articles, radio shows, and movies telling his story. He kept a list of friendly newspaper columnists, headed by Walter Winchell, who served as his eyes and ears. In turn, the director gave them useful tidbits of information to use against their rivals and enemies. He shaped the media through his backdoor favors and by parceling out his vast store of secrets.

Then he reached out to conservative organizations such as the American Legion, once again relying on them to pass back tips, and feeding them news about the Communist menace. Everywhere he went, he spread the message: Be afraid. Be on guard. Spies lurk all around. The FBI is your protector, for only we see everything; only we can outspy the spies.

In the late 1930s, Hoover began to speak out publicly, sharing his dark vision of an America under threat. One of Hoover's best biographers thinks a personal tragedy may have darkened the director's mood. For in 1938, his mother—his companion, the person with whom he had shared a home his entire life—died. Perhaps in some way, Annie's death freed him, for Hoover finally moved out of his childhood home and bought a new house in a better part of town. But in another way, his only truly intimate bond—his emotional umbilical chord—snapped. Cartha DeLoach, his longtime ally, was sure that when Annie died, "Hoover's capacity to feel deeply for other human beings" was buried with her.

From the late 1930s on, liberated by his understanding with FDR, driven perhaps by his own isolation, Hoover began his crusade against Communists, their "fellow travelers," their allies, and what he saw as their foolish friends.

There was, though, one group that was even more deceptive in its public statements than the FBI, and it was vastly more ruthless in its private actions: the Soviet Communists. The Communists were like a mirror image of Hoover and the FBI, but exaggerated to a grotesque and deadly degree. Hoover was often much more insightful than others about just how false-faced, calculating, and heartless the Soviet leader, Josef Stalin, could be. Perhaps he understood his enemy so well because he saw a glimpse of himself in that distant reflection.

Opposite: Hoover kept a photograph of his mother on his desk—just visible here behind the small lamp and pens. Her death, in 1938, may have ended his only deep emotional bond with another person.

PART FOUR

FACT: In 1932, Josef Stalin, general secretary of the Soviet Communist Party, became focused on building up industry and needed to buy machines from other countries. In order to get money, he decided to sell off the wheat crop grown in the Ukraine, which was then part of Soviet Russia. But he would have wheat to sell to foreigners only if he took it away from those who grew the grain and lived on the bread. Stalin hoarded and then exported so much wheat that approximately five million Ukrainians starved to death.

FACT: The Battle of Stalingrad, which lasted from August 1942 to February 1943, was a turning point of World War II. The Soviets lost perhaps a million soldiers defending the city, while some forty thousand civilians were killed in just one week. But by taking the immense losses, holding the city, and destroying the invading German army, the Soviets greatly weakened the Nazis, making the Allied victory possible.

The Fighting War

THE INSIDE STORY: The scale of death and destruction in the Soviet Union between 1930 and 1945 is beyond imagining. On the one hand, Stalin's forced famine in the Ukraine and his Great Terror killed millions. Some scholars consider the reign of death he inflicted on his own people comparable to Hitler's Holocaust. On the other hand, the Red Army accepted staggering losses in its determination to hold off and then defeat the Nazis. Depending on your point of view, you could see the Soviet Communists as the most callous murderers or the most self-sacrificing heroes. For many Ukrainian Americans, Stalin's murders were the ultimate crimes, and anti-Communism became a crusade. For many Jewish Americans, the Soviet role in fighting Hitler was the ultimate heroism, and anti-Communism was another form of anti-Semitism.

Background photograph: The siege of Stalingrad. The 2001 movie Enemy at the Gates *tells a fictionalized version of the story based on a real duel between rival snipers.*

As Stalin forced former heroes of the Soviet Union to make false confessions, his government erased them from the historical record, even scrubbing them out of photographs. Nikolai Yezhov was extremely loyal to Stalin and helped organize his murder campaign. But in 1940, when Stalin no longer found Yezhov useful, he was executed, and so no longer deserved to appear next to the Soviet leader.

10
GREAT INJUSTICE

By 1928, Josef Stalin (an invented name meaning "man of steel") had replaced Lenin as the head of the Soviet Union. Then, starting in 1936, something shifted in Stalin's mind. He became fearful, which forged his determination to find the "enemies of the working class" and "grind them down without stopping, without flagging." He meant exactly what he said. Stalin began to arrest, torture, convict, and murder his fellow Soviet citizens—and not just any old Communists. He set out to eliminate—that is, kill—the heroes of the 1917 Revolution, the very leaders who had been closest to Lenin. "We shall annihilate every one of these enemies," Stalin thundered, "even if he is an Old Bolshevik. We shall annihilate him and his relatives, his family. Any who in deed or in thought, yes, in thought, attacks the unity of the socialist state will be mercilessly crushed by us. We shall exterminate all enemies to the very last man, and also their families and relatives."

Stalin's murder campaign is known as the Great Terror or the "purge trials," since he was eliminating those he did not like from the Party. Those trials were a death sentence for the Americans who had rushed off to Russia to build the workers' state.

By 1938, school in Soviet Russia was no longer about calling classmates "comrade" and reading Mark Twain. Students were praised if they turned in their parents to the police, to be imprisoned or executed. Teenagers were taught to admire fourteen-year-old Pavlik Morozov, who told the police that his father was secretly keeping more than his share of grain. Young Communists competed to expose enemies of the state. And no one seemed more like a traitor to Communism than an American.

Pavlik Morozov was treated as a hero in the Soviet Union for turning his father in to the police to be executed, though he himself was soon murdered. Teenagers were encouraged to use him as their example and guide.

We met the Abolins when they left America to move to the Workers' Paradise (see chapter 8). Lucy Abolin's brothers and her father were handed over to the authorities, then executed. So-called trials would take ten minutes or less, and there was no appeal. No one in Russia would dare to disagree with a court verdict, because that would mean his or her own death sentence. Lucy's mother was sent off to a prison camp, where she, too, died.

Eliminating Americans was also a fine way to harvest documents. The Americans who had come to the Soviet Union to build Communism were asked—and often coerced—to give up their passports. This made it much harder for those who tired of Communism to leave. And as the Americans were executed, the government built up its hoard of passports to hand out to spies sent to America under false names.

Stalin's campaign of murder took approximately two million lives. But some Communists simply could not admit that the Soviets could be so vile. Paul Robeson was a great American singer, actor, and activist who was also a member of the American Communist Party. Though he never admitted that in public, he made no secret of his admiration for the Soviet Union. Robeson, who was said to be fluent in some twelve languages, would sing to miners in Wales, to factory workers in Russia, and to May Day crowds in America with the same booming bass voice, the same all-encompassing embrace. Listen to him sing, moving easily from Chinese to Russian to a black spiritual to Yiddish to a slightly amended English version of the "Ode to Joy," from the end of Beethoven's Ninth Symphony, and you cannot help sharing his vision of solidarity among all the peoples of the world.

Robeson was in Russia during the Great Terror. In a few cases, he did what he could to protect someone, to save a life. But when he was questioned about the deaths taking place all around him, he lied, denying what he knew to be true. Paul Robeson Jr. was in Russia with his father and could not help noticing that friends and their families were disappearing. In one instance, he confronted his father, saying, "We all knew he was innocent, and you never said a word." Paul Sr. felt that the cause of the people, the cause of Communism, was too important. He could not risk giving ammunition to its enemies. "Sometimes," he told his son, "great injustices may be inflicted on the minority when the majority is in the pursuit of a great and just cause."

The "great injustices" that left a trail of corpses and blood through the Soviet Union created the first of a series of crises for American Communists. Would they, like Paul Robeson, defend the cause either by denying Stalin's

Paul Robeson was just what this picture suggests—a larger-than-life man who sang for, spoke for, and believed in working people. Unfortunately, his strong beliefs made him unable to be truthful about what he saw going on in the Soviet Union.

crimes or, worse, by arguing that the millions of imprisoned or murdered Russians deserved their fate? Or would they break with Moscow, the homeland of the Communist ideal? In the name of science, Communism had turned into the most repressive religion, complete with its own Inquisition.

Stalin's drive to eliminate the heroes of 1917, followed by the reports of untold millions of deaths, forced American Communists into a stark choice: total commitment or total rejection. By 1937, one American Communist who had been such a believer in revolution that he was spying for the Soviets lost faith in the cause. And then on August 23, 1939, "Carl," as he called himself, received the most horrifying news: Stalin had signed a deal with Hitler. They agreed not to fight each other and, instead, to carve up Poland between them. For American leftists still wrestling with what to think of the Great Terror, this was the last straw. Anyone who had passed secrets on to Russia now knew that information might well be shared with Hitler. It was one thing to feel you were supporting the motherland of Communism; it was quite another to think you were spying for the Nazis. Carl approached FDR and the FBI, trying to pass on word of the spy cell he had helped to run in Washington. For the moment, no one would listen. But Carl's story was the hint of larger, deeper, shifts that were beginning to take place. Some Party members were losing faith, some allies of the Party were pulling away, and some who had felt bullied and intimidated by the Party were storing up their resentments. The Party of the future was becoming the mistake of the past. Hoover's moment to turn his fire against Communism was coming—but first there was a war to win.

11
HOOVER'S WAR

December 7, 1941, is a watershed date that every American should know, the day the Japanese attack on Pearl Harbor propelled America into World War II. But you could make the case that the more significant date in that same year was June 22. That was the day on which Hitler broke his alliance with Stalin and invaded Russia. In an instant, Russia went from being the Nazis' oil supplier to a crucial ally of Britain and the United States. Indeed, Russia took the brunt of the Nazi attack: while some three hundred thousand American soldiers would be killed during the war, Russia lost approximately nine million soldiers and perhaps nineteen million civilians. Russia gave everything it had to defeat the Nazis.

You can forgive American leftists and Communists for a moment of whiplash; they went from having to defend Stalin's pact with Hitler to announcements of U.S.-U.S.S.R. solidarity. The sudden warming of relations between Moscow and Washington was good news for Soviet spies. Americans who passed information on to Soviet handlers could once again feel they were helping an ally, a close cousin in the fight against fascism. But Hoover did not trust the Russians. Convincing the public that it was safe under the watchful eyes of the FBI was one of his main goals during the war.

Hoover's first big opportunity began in the dead of night on June 13, 1942. John Cullen, a Coast Guardsman patrolling a beach on the far eastern tip of Long Island, New York, noticed four men battling the waves to land a raft. According to *The FBI Story,* one of the men looked directly at Cullen and snarled, "How old are you? Do you have a father and mother? I don't want to kill you. You don't know what this is all about. Why don't you forget it? Here is some money. Go out and have yourself a good time."

Cullen knew something was very wrong. One of the men had started to speak in German. Looking out at the water, Cullen could just discern a long, thin object that could be the ridgeline of a submarine. Were the Nazis invading? The Guardsman managed to get away and rushed off to tell his superiors—who at first didn't believe him. Eventually, the Coast Guard went back to the beach, where they found explosives, blasting caps, and even German uniforms buried in the sand. But by then the four men—who were indeed Nazis sent to America to blow up bridges and spread fear—had taken the first train to New York City. By noon, Hoover learned that four saboteurs were on the loose somewhere, perhaps in America's largest and most vulnerable city.

As Hoover wanted the story to be told, the next few days showed his FBI at its best. Apparently George Dasch, leader of the Nazi crew, and his partner Ernest Berger got cold feet. *The FBI Story* says that "in their hearts they knew they were hunted men. They were well aware that death was the usual penalty for wartime espionage. . . . Their courage was oozing away." To this day, the official FBI history website proposes that Dasch may have feared that the project would fail and wanted to confess before someone else did and he got caught. But Dasch himself later claimed that he had never intended to go through with the plot, that he was on America's side all along. In the Hoover version, the closing noose of the ever-vigilant G-men scared an enemy into confessing. According to Dasch, he kept trying to turn himself in, and the FBI turned him away.

When Dasch called the New York office of the FBI and said he was a Nazi spy, the officer figured he was just another nut job wasting the Bureau's time and answered, "Yesterday Napoleon called." Dasch grabbed a suitcase crammed with packets of dollar bills and boarded the next train to Washington. If he could not get the New York office to take him seriously, he was going to find Hoover himself. But headquarters was no more receptive to a strange man claiming to be a spy than was New York. The leader of the German plot was shunted from one office to another until he was finally face-to-face with D. M. Ladd, the man who was leading the nationwide manhunt for the spy team. Alas, not even Ladd could believe Dasch's wild story. Desperate to convince these thickheaded bureaucrats that he was who he said he was, Dasch "seized the suitcase that had been lying on the floor, tore its snaps, and dumped the contents on the desk." Some eighty-four thousand dollars in cash cascaded over the wooden top and onto the floor.

The spy-who-never-wanted-to-be-a-spy finally managed to convince the agency-that-didn't-want-to-listen that the most wanted man in America was sitting right in front of them. Over the next eight days, Dasch talked and talked and talked. Not only did he lead the FBI to another team of four Germans who had landed successfully in Florida; he also described the entire Nazi sabotage plot in great detail.

By June 27, a headline in the New York *Daily News* broadcast the great news: "FBI Captures 8 German Agents Landed by Subs." According to Hoover, and later accounts approved by him, teamwork, diligence, and science had triumphed. Dasch's relentless determination to turn himself in was carefully erased—just as the story of Melvin Purvis, superagent, had disappeared from the record. Indeed, when the Germans were tried in a secret military court, they were all sentenced to death. Inexplicably, Dasch and Berger had their sentences reduced to thirty years' hard labor. Only after the war, and against Hoover's objections, did Dasch's story come to light. In 1948, he was deported to Germany. He was a free man but was still treated as a spy, not a hero, by the American government.

Even though the story of the invincible FBI swooping in on the Nazi saboteurs was not true, it served a good purpose during the war. The rapid

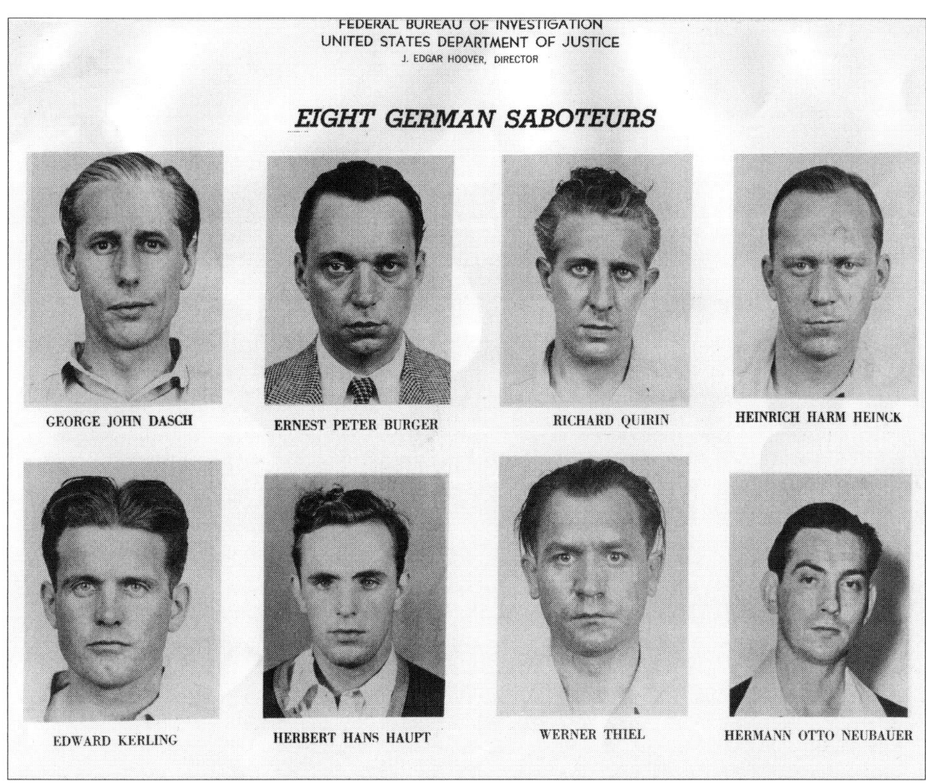

The eight Nazis who landed on Long Island. Dasch and Burger turned themselves in and were returned to Germany after the war.

capture of the two submarine teams may well have convinced the Nazis to cancel their sabotage campaign. According to Dasch, they had planned to land terrorists by submarine every six weeks. But after the first failure, the Germans dropped the idea. As ever, Hoover won as much through the public image he created as by the actual accomplishments of his men.

DETECT, DETAIN, CONTROL

Hoover believed in one basic strategy for dealing with threats: identify people who might be dangerous; detain them; project peace, calm, and control to the public at large. National security counted more than personal freedom—as long as that judgment was made on a case-by-case basis by a careful, informed, professional such as J. Edgar Hoover. Hoover asked his key officers to compile lists of Americans with "German, Italian, and Communist sympathies." At a word, these citizens were to be swept into "custodial detention"—jailed on the authority of the FBI. Hoover decided who might be a threat—which meant that the FBI began to secretly investigate moderate black civil rights organizations such as the NAACP.

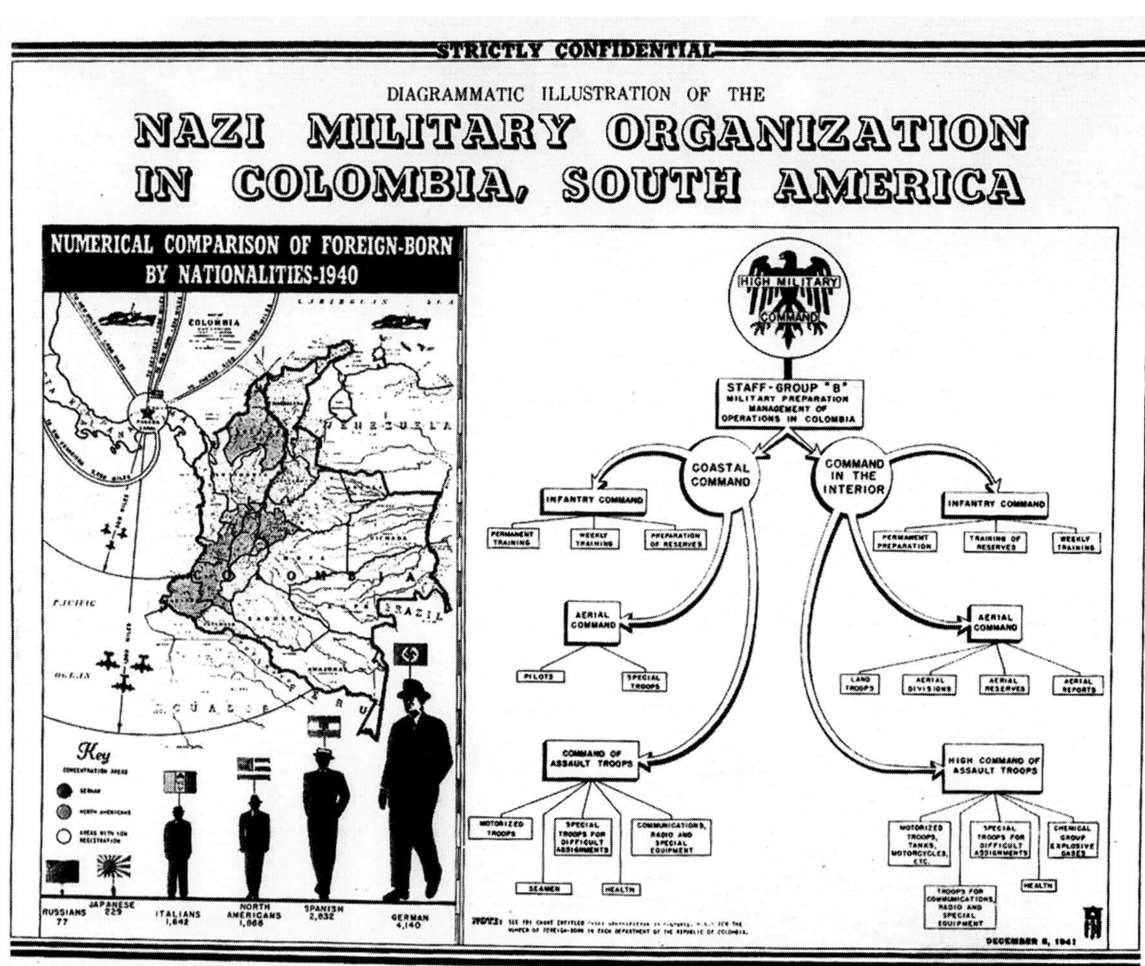

Hoover's FBI was ahead of its time in crafting clear, readable graphs and charts that showed the challenges it faced and its striking record of success. As ever, Hoover was a master of impeccable presentation—here detailing the Bureau's wartime work against Nazis in South America.

The detention list made perfect sense to Hoover: know your enemy and control him. But it was not legal. In 1943, a new attorney general (and thus technically his boss), Francis Biddle, explicitly told Hoover that. But the director was sure he was right. So while he ordered all his agents to drop the idea of custodial detention, he also instructed them to maintain the very same lists, now called the Security Index. Just like his Do Not File file, the Security Index was "strictly confidential." The attorney general would see that Hoover had obeyed his order to get rid of lists of people to round up. He would not know that custodial detention had been replaced by an identical, though hidden, scheme under a different name.

The key to Hoover's plan was information—like the file cards he had started back in 1919. But the very fact that he trusted his superior knowledge made him oppose the most infamous World War II detention program: the internment of Japanese Americans. "I thought the army was getting a bit hysterical," he complained to the head of his San Francisco office. He believed there could be only "one efficient method of processing the Japanese for loyalty, which consists of individual, not mass, consideration." Hoover wanted files with names, dates, and concrete allegations. Identifying, plucking out, and neutralizing specific individuals reflected the wisdom and efficiency of the FBI. Mass arrests were clumsy—that was the lesson of the Palmer raids. Hoover was ruthless, devious, and power hungry. He was not clumsy.

Hoover's war was his career in miniature: he had real successes, propaganda successes, and illegal plots he hid from his superiors. He was always fighting on two fronts: to defeat real enemies and to shape how others saw the battle. "We must clean up democracy at home while watching for threats to it from abroad," he warned. The country needed to toughen up because, he was sure, there was a secret danger looming: "the Communist virus." Only a strong nation firm in its values could guard against the infection of evil. When the fighting war ended, Hoover would begin the real conflict—against his mirror image: the ruthless, devious, and power-hungry Communists.

PART FIVE

FACT: On April 12, 1945, President Roosevelt, recently elected for an unprecedented fourth term, died. Two months earlier, even as his body was failing, he had met with Stalin and Prime Minister Winston Churchill of England to map out the borderlines of the postwar world. FDR's death left Harry Truman as president, and those who had long mistrusted the Communists and despised FDR saw their opportunity.

FACT: From 1938 on, a congressional committee, the House Committee on Un-American Activities (HUAC), held hearings attempting to show Communist influences in government, in Hollywood, and in the State Department. After the war ended and several former spies (including "Carl," whose real name was Whittaker Chambers) confessed, HUAC hearings became a media circus and drew national attention.

The War of Shadows

THE INSIDE STORY: President Truman did not trust HUAC or the House Republicans who kept bringing up the "Reds in Washington" story. He believed they were trying to whip up fear in order to attack FDR's legacy and as a cynical tool to win elections. But by 1947, he realized that he was on the wrong side of a popular issue. Truman announced that everyone who worked for the government would have to prove their loyalty by swearing an oath that they were not, and had never been, members of the Communist Party. It was legal to belong to the Communist Party, but if you did, the oath put you in a bind. Admit you were a Communist, and you might well be fired. Hide your past or your beliefs, and if Hoover or HUAC or anyone else found out, you would be prosecuted for lying.

Background photograph: An American atomic bomb being exploded on Bikini Island, in the Pacific, on July 25, 1946. Tests such as this were designed to show the power of the nations that had atomic weapons, but they also spread the mood of fear. The mushroom cloud the blasts produced became a symbol of the destruction

Whittaker Chambers, at the microphone, was the former Communist code-named Carl who tried to turn himself in to both FDR's key assistant and the FBI. In 1948, he publicly accused Alger Hiss, one of the planners of the United Nations and an honored public official during the New Deal, of having been a fellow Communist and even a fellow spy. Hiss was ultimately convicted of perjury, but for generations Americans continued to take sides for and against him. The photo shows Chambers testifying to the House Committee on Un-American Activities (HUAC), whose hearings split the nation: were the Democrats protecting Communists, or were the Republicans trying to attack FDR's record by linking him to Stalin's Russia?

12
THE HOPE OF THE WORLD

On August 29, 1949, the Soviet Union exploded its first atomic bomb. How could that be? Atomic science was America's secret, created with the cooperation of England and Canada, our partners in freedom. We had beaten the Nazis to the bomb. But now the Soviets were our main threat. How had this genie gotten out of the bottle? Hoover was certain that spies had stolen key information. But who were they? The Soviets first learned that America was trying to create an atomic bomb in 1941. They immediately created a mission, code-named Enormous, to learn over the Americans' shoulders. "Enormous" referred, of course, to the power of the bomb, but it also signaled the scale of the Soviet effort; they were desperate to know what the Americans were doing. Now Hoover needed to untangle the web of spies the Soviets had spun.

The FBI's best agents scrambled to solve "the crime of the century." The Bureau found one hint in a captured Nazi file, another in the confession of a captured Soviet agent. The trail pointed to Klaus Fuchs, a German atomic scientist living in England. Fuchs was first questioned in January of 1950, and by February he broke. Tracing his connections soon yielded a cluster of American atomic spies: Harry Gold, who had gathered information from Fuchs and given it to the Russians; David Greenglass, a skilled machinist who worked at a base where the American bomb was first tested; and Greenglass's brother-in-law, Julius Rosenberg.

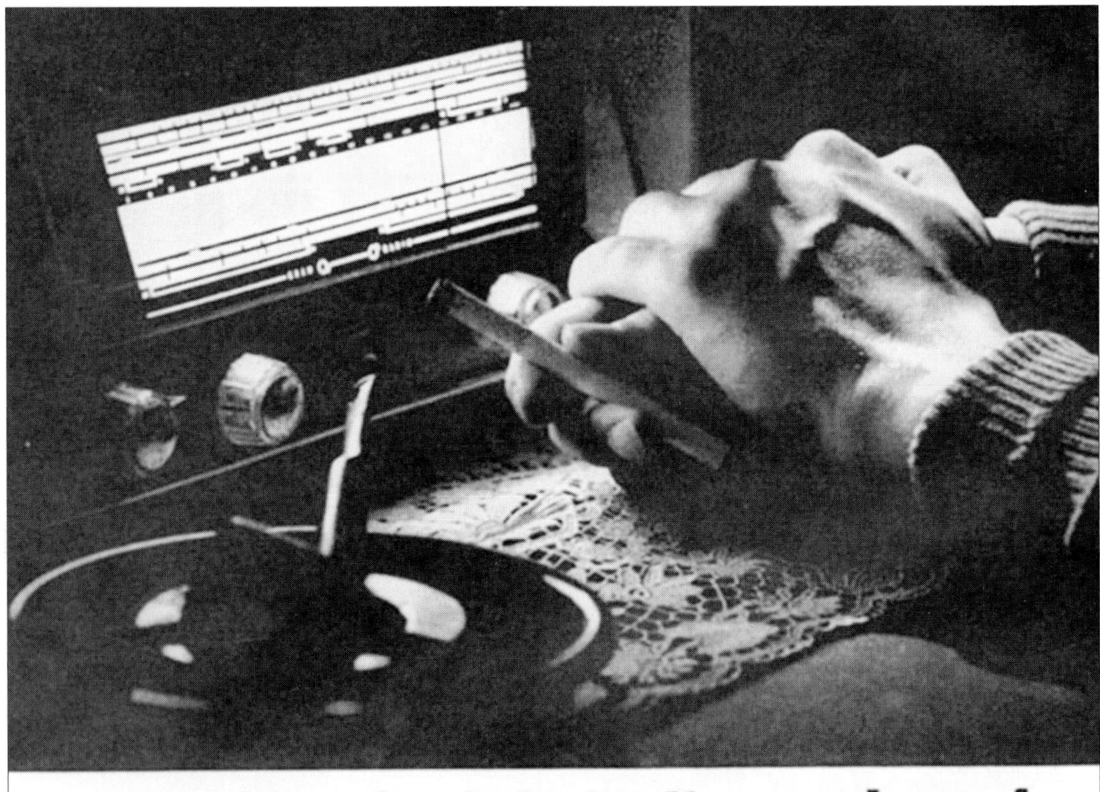

In the 1950s, radio was a key tool used to communicate across borders. The American government used Radio Free Europe to undermine the Soviets. Yet in America, young people were listening, late at night, to rock 'n' roll, which made them question the segregated daylight world.

Rosenberg was a committed Communist who had eagerly passed on whatever information he could to the Soviets. He was married to David Greenglass's sister, Ethel. In 1944, as luck would have it, Greenglass was assigned to the secret testing ground at Los Alamos, New Mexico. Julius and Ethel sat down with David's wife, Ruth, and had an earnest conversation. Julius asked "how she felt about the Soviet Union and how deep in general did her Communist convictions go." She "replied without hesitation that to her Socialism was the only hope of the world and the Soviet Union commanded her deepest admiration."

There are two ways to see that most private conversation. Looking at the world in 1944 through Communist eyes, you saw Russians sacrificing untold millions of their citizens to defeat Hitler. You believed that only by joining the workers of the world together, by uniting the common people, could the hell of war lead to a better future. You saw an America whose own armies were racially segregated, that interned Japanese-American citizens; an England that clung to its empire and denied people of color in India, Africa, and the Caribbean the right to their own nations; and you saw these two nations developing a weapon of unimaginable power. You would believe it was your duty as a humanist, as a world citizen, to share what you knew with the Soviet Union, the nation devoted to the rights and dreams of the working people. Indeed, after the war, many of the scientists who developed the bomb argued that the technology was so dangerous, it should be controlled by an international body; it could not belong to any one nation. Julius and Ethel, Ruth and David, could all feel that they were merely ensuring that the capitalists, the imperialists, would not rule the earth. In their minds, they were idealists, not traitors.

If you looked at precisely that same kitchen-table conversation another way, you saw that the Soviets were the most heartless liars. They murdered millions of their own people, and used dreamers like Ruth as pawns. They wanted the bomb solely to shore up their own power. If the Rosenbergs and Greenglasses were idealists, they were also foolish. And they were citizens not of some vague world union of working people but of the United States. At best they were completely misguided. At worst they were vile traitors.

In June 1950, the FBI arrested Julius and Ethel. The national mood about their forthcoming trial was influenced by events outside America, where the shadows of evil seemed to be growing ever longer.

In October 1949, homegrown Communists completed their takeover of China. Earlier in the century, American missionaries had been hopeful that China would soon turn Christian. Now it had gone in completely the opposite direction—to atheistic Marxism. The very next year, war broke out in Korea. Communists in the north, supported by the Soviets, invaded the south, and America was taken by surprise. Why was Asia slipping away? Why was America, the winner of World War II, stumbling, facing new threats everywhere? The Rosenberg case suggested one clear answer: spies had infiltrated the government and were secretly handing this country over to their masters. The House Committee on Un-American Activities, it seemed to many, was not a political organ out to undermine Democrats. Rather, the Democrats were trying to cover up their blunders in being "soft" on Communism.

As ever, Hoover wanted information. If he could get Julius to talk, it would allow the FBI to "proceed against other individuals." But Julius was not cooperating, so Hoover suggested a way to get him to open up. "Proceedings against his wife might serve as a lever in this matter." To Hoover, the question was not whether Ethel was guilty but whether threatening her might get Julius to confess and name other conspirators. The tactic failed.

Both of the Rosenbergs insisted that they were innocent, which also meant they refused to answer questions about other spies. Their defiance turned the question of how to judge them into the most public debate.

Should they be seen as idealists or traitors? As foolish or heartless? Were they equally guilty, or was Julius the spy and Ethel merely his silent and accommodating wife? What price should they pay for passing on information that may have been useful to the Soviets?

The Rosenbergs were convicted of spying. As Judge Irving Kaufman debated what sentence to hand down, he asked for Hoover's opinion. The director was oddly protective of Ethel. She was the mother of two small children, someone the public would rally around and seek to protect. But Judge Kaufman was determined to send the clearest and most absolute message. He ruled that the Rosenbergs had committed a crime "worse than murder." "Millions more of innocent people," he warned, "may pay the price of your treason." And so he decided that they both must be executed, in the electric chair.

Just as the Hiss-Chambers confrontations split the public, so did the Rosenberg trial. Were they master-spy traitors whose crimes showed the need for ever more government vigilance or victims of anti-Semitic selective prosecution whose execution was a dangerous sign of the rise of American fascism?

Hoover was right about one side of the public's reaction to the death sentence. Artists, intellectuals, and leftists throughout the world protested for the Rosenbergs, for their young sons, and against the judge's decision. But to another sector of the American public, the lineup of liberal defenders only made the Rosenbergs more suspect.

The Rosenbergs were slated to be executed on June 18, 1953. That night, as the defense tried its last appeals, hundreds of supporters kept vigil outside the White House. They were hoping to pressure President Eisenhower to let the Rosenbergs live. Just across Pennsylvania Avenue, "a tremendous crowd

Opposite: What if your nice, normal neighbors are not whom they seem to be? This 1956 movie played on people's fears of what lay beneath the facade of conformity.

gathered, smelling blood. They booed and screamed at us." At the moment when the Rosenbergs were to die, those siding with the Rosenbergs put down their signs and "silently faced the White House. The crowd across the street shrieked with joy."

Protesters gathering before traveling to the White House to urge President Eisenhower to stop the execution of the Rosenbergs. While it is not clear in this distant shot, the crowd was interracial. The conflict over the Rosenberg case—in which they were probably both guilty—was also a clash over what it meant to be an American.

Why would a crowd "shriek with joy" at the news that a couple has died? Ethel was accused of being a bad mother, because she had a job. Communists were often said to have loose sexual lives. They were seen as perverts, out to corrupt children. To fearful Americans in the early 1950s, Communism represented everything that endangered a simple, happy American way of life. Americans were scared of the Soviets and the Red Chinese, scared of the atomic bomb and what seemed like the real possibility of World War III, scared of the spies who seemed to have infiltrated Washington; some were scared of their own pasts, when they had marched in Communist parades or even condemned their neighbors for not supporting Communist causes.

In this time of fear, the anti-Communists were on the march and out to crush, to stamp out, to extinguish their enemies. Hoover finally had his chance to clean out the Communist infection so that America would be safe, quiet, untroubled by strikes or protests against racism, and guarded by the growing file cards of the ever-vigilant FBI.

The FBI was everywhere. Between 1945 and 1953, you could listen to *This Is Your FBI* on radio, and if your local boys' club hosted an FBI night, they might get mentioned on the air. In 1948, Hoover helped Hollywood make *The Street with No Name,* a crime drama about the Bureau, and used his lists of friendly press contacts to promote it. Two years later, the FBI started its Ten Most Wanted list. It was tacked up in every post office, reminding people to be scared, and simultaneously assuring them that G-men were watching.

There is always some reason to be afraid—whether that is because teenagers claim to be under attack from witches in Salem in 1692, or bombs explode in Washington in 1919, or Communist spies turn over atomic secrets thirty-five years later, or airplanes fly into the World Trade Center in 2001, or indeed whatever rumor rushes through a school today. But when personal worries are confirmed by police raids, congressional hearings, judges' rulings, presidential decrees, newspaper headlines, gossip-column tidbits, and the whispers of government agents, the nation freezes.

In the early 1950s, Hoover was the center of a vast network of FBI agents, former agents, policemen, retired soldiers, newsmen, and religious leaders who shared his fears: they were all on guard against invisible microbes—of disease, of ideas, and of "perverted" desire. Hoover's hidden network was the deep structure of the fearful '50s: the age of Senator Joseph McCarthy.

13
TAILGUNNER JOE

A hardscrabble farm boy from rural Wisconsin who hustled his way through law school, then served as a marine during World War II, Joseph McCarthy made his own breaks. He was the face of men who'd grown up in the Great Depression and fought in the war; they knew what it took to get by in a hard, tough world. No one expected McCarthy to win when he ran for the Senate in 1946. But he defied the experts: he invented a record of wartime heroism and was such an energetic campaigner that he was elected. At thirty-eight, he was the youngest member of the Senate, yet that success only made him hungry for more attention, more power, and more glory. McCarthy's need to be liked was so strong, it radiated around him like heat. As one senator recalled, he was "like a mongrel dog, fawning on you one moment and the next moment trying to bite your leg off." His hungers had no limits—which is why he rose so far and so fast. And behind the scenes, where no one could see, Hoover fed him his lines. Take the speech that made McCarthy famous.

February 9, 1950. Senator Joe McCarthy was the scheduled speaker at a minor event in a minor city: a Republican women's club meeting in Wheeling, West Virginia. "The Democratic Christian world," Wisconsin's junior senator warned, was in grave peril. And Joe knew the secret behind the rise of the forces of evil: "The reason why we find ourselves in a position of impotency is not because the enemy has sent men to invade our shores, but rather because of the traitorous actions of those . . . who have had all the benefits that the wealthiest nation on earth has had to offer — the finest homes, the finest college educations, and the finest jobs in Government we can give."

Anyone who had followed the chase for the A-bomb spies knew exactly what the rough-hewn senator was speaking about. Smooth-talking traitors had oozed into high government office, then steered the nation off course. It took a guy like McCarthy to tell the foul truth and to put the country right. McCarthy didn't mind hard work. As a teenager he'd started his own little chicken farm and was known "as the only man who could go out to the barn on a cold winter night wearing two coats and come back with chicken droppings all over the outside coat and the inside one as well." Now, in Wheeling, he was wading into the muck again. Maybe he'd get splattered, maybe he'd look dirty, but damned if he wouldn't clean out the henhouse. McCarthy's exact words have been lost to history, but he held up a piece of paper and said something like "I have here in my hand a list of 205 people working in the State Department who have been named as members of the Communist Party and members of a spy ring."

McCarthy was making it up; there was nothing on that piece of paper. Pressed to show his famous list, he always seemed to have left it in his luggage. And he quickly adjusted his numbers from 205 to 207 to 81 to 57. McCarthy took a gambler's chance: he slapped

Mickey Spillane's novels were the most popular books in America; they featured he-man heroes and a silent, efficient FBI. Many were made into films.

the Democrats, FDR's legacy, and the State Department across the face, and dared anyone to hit back, to prove him wrong. Senate Democrats obliged, charging a bipartisan committee headed by Millard Tydings, a Democrat from Maryland, with the task of making McCarthy show his evidence or admit his lies. Frantic, McCarthy called in his backup.

According to William Sullivan, then an assistant director at the FBI, Hoover was McCarthy's secret source. "The FBI," he later wrote, "kept Joe McCarthy in business. . . . We gave McCarthy all we had." The network of former agents, reporters, and authors Hoover cultivated rushed to help out, as did the young congressman Richard Nixon. While Hoover's men scoured their lists to find some real Communists in the State Department, the director's allies crafted McCarthy's speeches. McCarthy grabbed the moment. He was thrilled to be the exterminator who was going to rip off the rotting wood in Washington and force the insectlike Commie spies to scatter.

At the end of February, the head of the State Department's own security team assured Congress that it had already removed 202 "security risks." Ninety-one of these employees lost their jobs, even though there was no evidence that they had ever been pro-Communist. Instead, they were fired because they were said to be homosexuals. Looming beneath the fear that Communists had infiltrated Washington was the even deeper concern that "perverts" were weakening our nation and our government from within.

Why the concern over homosexuals? During the busy days of the New Deal and the hectic war years, single men and women rushed to Washington to find work. Naturally enough, the city provided relatively open meeting places for

This 1951 exposé claimed that there were more than six thousand homosexuals in government and that these "dumb, dull deviates" ruled the city through their "femmocracy." The authors combined fear of homosexuality with resentment of a growing government in tough language people enjoyed reading. The book was an instant hit, selling more than 150,000 copies in its first three weeks and reaching number one on the New York Times *bestseller list.*

The F.B.I. knew those two code experts were fruity fellows, but nothing was done about it until the boys had already minced off to Moscow. How many more pansies do we have, in strategic positions, whose perverted pursuits in hotel rooms have been caught on cameras by cunning Commie agents, to be used as blackmail bait to make the homos turn against their homeland?

Behind The Scandal Of Those Two Traitors:

HOW THE REDS BLACKMAIL HOMOSEXUALS INTO SPYING FOR THEM!

William H. Martin (left) and Bernon F. Mitchell, the two lavender lads who were code experts for the U.S. before becoming turncoats and flitting off to Russia.

BY JAMES SHAWCROSS

THE recent case of the two American defectors — or, to put it more bluntly, traitors — who went over to the Reds after slipping away from their work at a super-secret U. S. security agency, has come as a great shock to many people.

No one could understand how two young men like these — clean-cut fellows who looked like typical all-American boys — could betray their own homeland to the Russians. After all, these men came from solid, church-going families, lived in the kind of small towns for which this country is famous, and seemed as safe from subversion as two young men could be.

You've read about this case in the newspapers and heard about it on the air. But the BIG TRUTH behind it has not yet been told!

For the truth is this:

The Reds are using a new tactic in recruiting spies and traitors, and it's working. The new tactic is to gain access to American secrets by using — homosexuals!

It is a pattern that is becoming familiar to Western counter-espionage agents. The Reds trap these twilight men in indiscretions and then blackmail them. They tell the homosexual that if he won't give the information they want, they'll see that he's exposed in his sex peculiarity.

It was thru two highly vulnerable characters of this ilk that the Russians were able to get access to documents in the hush-hush National Security Agency.

The treason of two NSA code experts, Bernon F. Mitchell and William H. Martin, finally brought into action all the agencies of government that SHOULD have been on the job long ago. And the investigations by these agencies — and especially by Congress—have turned up material that's so explosive they'll never be able to suppress it, try as they may.

Maybe the government gumshoes who're supposed to look after security matters just aren't hip enough. Ask any Washington correspondent, or any alert (and normal) man in the capital, for that matter, and he'll tell you that this is an old, old problem in Miss Liberty's home town on the Potomac.

Back in World War II, for example, one of the top men in the State Department was widely known as a homosexual, and yet he was untouchable. Let one lavender lad get into a place, and before you know it the place is swarming with limp-wristed "boys" who couldn't wiggle their hips more if they were Marilyn Monroe (which they wish they were). And that's what happened at State. The place was crawling with fairies, but there was nothing good about this kind of fairy. Most of the agencies in Washington have been afflicted with this curse at one time or another, to the dismay of the government girls.

Throughout Washington, Prince Georges County in adjacent Maryland, and parts of Virginia just across the Potomac, there are scores of places that cater almost exclusively to homosexuals. The fairies call them "gay" joints. Some are night clubs specializing in female impersonators, some are simply bars and grills, and some are apparently innocuous restaurants.

These joints are heavily patronized —so heavily that you sometimes can't elbow your way into them — and the patrons fall into two groups (which is a ducky idea, from their somewhat warped point of view):

1) The homosexuals, living it up.

2) The Russian agents, setting their snares.

In dimly lit cocktail lounges and in the glare of fluorescence in less subtle homo hangouts, the agents strike up conversations with men they've been watching, men who seem to work for the government but don't say what agency. This is the telltale sign of the man who works for a secret agency and has security clearance. For a standing rule at all the hush-hush security agencies — NSA, Central Intelligence Agency, and the like — is: Never tell anyone you work here.

The agents proposition the eager homo, and off he goes with them to a private room where anything can (and does) happen. But what the homo doesn't know, until too late, is that hidden cameras have photo-

Aerial view of the grounds of the National Security Agency, at Fort Meade, Maryland, which was a very hush-hush agency — until these two spies queered things.

14

Bernon Mitchell and William Martin were indeed American intelligence experts who fled to the Soviet Union. But they were not lovers and had not been blackmailed by the Communists. Fear of Russian influence, homosexual secrets, and growing government blurred together in sensational stories like this one.

all kinds of mutual attraction. The backlash against that tolerant Washington was one more way postwar Americans were trying to erase, and clean up, their pasts. But there was another, more personal, side to the campaign to get homosexuals out of government. A national survey of college-educated white men first published in 1948 reported that more than a third had had at least one homosexual experience. This was completely at odds with the dominant images of American masculinity. The Kinsey Report, as the survey was known, fed the unease of the time. What lurked within Washington, the government, or a person's own past and secret desires? A passion for the wrong ideas? Or the wrong person?

By 1952, McCarthy had set up his own echo of Hoover's files of illegally obtained information. He even boasted about it: "I have instructed a vast number of federal employees that they are duty-bound to give me information even though some little bureaucrat has stamped it 'secret' to defend himself." In other words, Senator McCarthy instructed government employees to break the law, steal material they were not allowed to see or share, and pass it along to him.

After conducting his investigation, Tydings called McCarthy a "fraud" whose accusations were nothing more than street-corner gossip. "You," he told his fellow senators, "will find out who has been whitewashing—with mud and slime, with filth, with the dregs of publicity at the expense of the people's love for their country. I ask the Senate: What are you going to do about it?"

The Senate split along party lines. Republicans supported McCarthy, and Democrats condemned him. And that fall, when Tydings ran for reelection, McCarthy did his worst. He blended a photo of Tydings with a completely different one of the head of the American Communist Party so that it looked as if they were in close conversation. The caption said it was a "composite," but at a glance, Tydings seemed to be good friends with a known Communist. Money secretly contributed by Texas oilmen covered the costs of distributing the doctored photo far and wide. Tydings lost badly, and McCarthy enjoyed his revenge on the man who had called his bluff.

Bullies fight dirty; they want their victims to look weak and foolish. That was McCarthy's gift: he was so unscrupulous, so determined to win, that he simply ignored any rules of fairness or even logic. The fighting marine just attacked, and attacked, and attacked. As one Republican senator said to him, "You're a real SOB. But sometimes it's useful to have SOBs around to do the dirty work." Joe was such an obvious blowhard that his critics were either horrified or terrified: horrified that he could behave so badly, terrified when his coarse, crude lies proved to be immensely popular.

Anyone could see that McCarthy kept changing his accusations, hammering at his enemies with the vaguest evidence. But for a lot of Americans who felt they had paid their dues in poverty and war and wanted a safe, normal, happy life, that was just fine. Joe McCarthy wasn't one to wait around for the enemy to attack or to gather every little fact about egghead conspirators; he was going to pound first and ask questions later. As McCarthy put it, one of his childhood chores had been to "dig out and destroy" skunks. "It was a dirty, foul, unpleasant, smelly job. And sometimes after it was done, people did not like us to sit next to them in church." That was just like exposing Communists. Joe might bend some rules, speak too loud, beat up the wrong guy. He might wrinkle some noses in the rare air of the Senate. McCarthy didn't care. "Some people," he said, "have told me that I shouldn't get so rough. . . . As long as I am in the United States Senate . . . I don't intend to treat traitors like gentlemen." For the people who liked McCarthy and hated Commie skunks, half-dirty accusations that were half true were true enough. That left the one woman in the Senate to challenge him.

Margaret Chase Smith of Maine was a moderate Republican and quite ready to believe that Communists and homosexuals had infiltrated the State Department. But she could not abide Joe's wild-swinging accusations. He was a barroom brawler, and she was a New England lady. And so, on June 1,

Opposite: The large image is the composite photo McCarthy supporters used to smear Senator Tydings in his reelection campaign. It purports to show the senator (right) listening to Gus Hall, head of the American Communist Party. The two smaller pictures are the original images from which the composite was made.

Twelve years after her Declaration of Conscience, Margaret Chase Smith ran for the Republican Party nomination for president, the first time a woman had sought the nomination from either major party. She lost to the eventual candidate, Senator Barry Goldwater.

1950, she stood up in the Senate and made her declaration of conscience. "The American people," she insisted, "are sick and tired of being afraid to speak their minds lest they be politically smeared as 'Communists' or 'Fascists' by their opponents. Freedom of speech is not what it used to be in America." In the heat of the anti-Communist fury, basic American rights were being lost: "The right to criticize; the right to hold unpopular beliefs; the right to protest; the right of independent thought. The exercise of these rights should not cost one single American citizen his reputation or his right to a livelihood nor should he be in danger of losing his reputation or livelihood merely because he happens to know someone who holds unpopular beliefs. Who of us doesn't? Otherwise none of us could call our souls our own. Otherwise thought control would have set in."

Senator Smith defined America as a place of argument, dissent, and protest, not a land to be governed by fear and "thought control." She was exactly like Louis Post protecting innocent immigrants from deportation. But at the time, almost all her Senate colleagues abandoned her. McCarthy was too popular, and McCarthyism—angry anti-Communism—was a tide no one wanted to buck.

When McCarthy, with rising polls at his back, clashed with Smith, the voice of conscience, Hoover not only fed documents to the rabid senator; he also doctored some of them so that they could not be traced back to the FBI. If we look back with the eyes of a historian, we might say that McCarthy was a lying bully; Hoover was a deceitful, manipulative lawbreaker; Smith, Tydings, and the citizens who dared to join with them were the heroes. That is where the story used to end. But there is still another layer to this war of shadows, and it was not revealed until the 1990s. Beneath this evident clash between liars and people of conscience lay one more secret chamber. In fact, there had been far more Communist spies in Washington than liberals wanted to admit, and the man who knew that, for sure, was J. Edgar Hoover.

VENONA

Soviet spies in America needed to communicate with their handlers back home, so they devised what should have been a perfect system. Each message was encoded, then encrypted by a method that would be used only once. Even if every single message was intercepted—and in fact that did happen for three years—there should have been no patterns for the Americans to analyze. Each message would have its own unique secret key. So, for example, if every cable read "Hello. How are you? I am fine. The spying is going well today," a person who intercepted it would have no way to know what that meant, since each day every single letter, space, or punctuation mark could mean something different. "A" might be a letter one day, a number the next, and a placeholder on the third.

VENONA

~~TOP SECRET~~

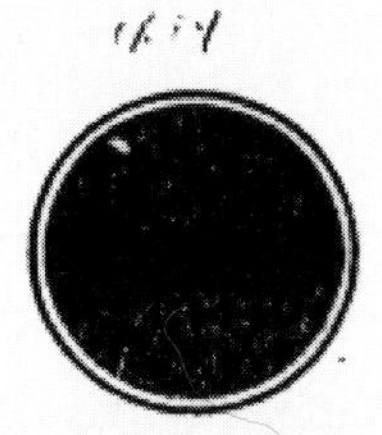

USSR

Ref. No.:

Issued : 25/6/1973

Copy No.: 301

MEETING BETWEEN "GUS'" AND "REST"; WORK ON ENORMOUS (1944)

From: NEW YORK

To: MOSCOW

No.: 195 9th February 1944

Personal to VIKTOR[i].

In reply to No. 302[ii].

On 5th February a meeting took place between "GUS'"[iii] and "REST"[iv]. Beforehand GUS' was given a detailed briefing by us. REST greeted him pleasantly but was rather cautious at first, [1 group unrecovered] the discussion GUS' satisfied himself that REST was aware of whom he was working with. R.[iv] arrived in the COUNTRY[STRANA][v] in September as a member of the ISLAND[OSTROV][vi] mission on ENORMOUS[ENORMOZ][vii]. According to him the work on ENORMOUS in the COUNTRY is being carried out under the direct control of the COUNTRY's army represented by General SOMERVELL[SOMMERVILL][viii] and STIMSON[ix]: at the head of the group of ISLANDERS[OSTROVITYaNE][vi] is a Labour Member of Parliament, Ben SMITH[x].

[Continued overleaf]

VENONA

TOP SECRET

But by 1943, the Americans, aided by the British, learned that the Communists had been sloppy; they were getting such a flood of information that they sometimes reused the same encoding pattern. With three years of extremely careful and painstaking work, the code breakers of the Venona Project began to be able to read the Soviet cables. Some 2,900 notes originally sent between 1940 and 1948 were decoded; they are now on the Internet for anyone to read. But at the time, Venona was a top-secret project.

By 1948, Hoover knew about the Venona decryptions. President Truman, current evidence suggests, was never told. In each of the big flashpoint cases of the period — the revelations from "Carl" and other former spies, the Rosenberg trials and protests — Hoover knew more than the president.

As long as the Venona Project was active, it could not, of course, be made public. If the Soviets knew that the Americans had cracked their code, they would change it, as indeed they did when William Weisband, an American Communist who actually worked on the Venona Project, managed to pass on word of what was going on. But that meant that when liberal critics attacked testimony given in court, they were seeing only the tip of the iceberg. When Hoover claimed that the American Communist Party was the pawn of Stalin's plan to undermine and ultimately overturn the government of the United States, he was not being a prisoner of his fears; he was passing along the essence of the secret that Venona revealed. The American Communist Party, as a very recent history book that incorporates the Venona decryptions makes clear, was an "auxiliary service to Soviet intelligence."

Hoover, and even McCarthy, were right in some particulars: there were more spies in government than FDR's administration cared to know about when "Carl" contacted them in 1939 or than Truman believed when his Republican enemies attacked him as soft on Communism eight years later. The Republicans were using the issue of Communism as a political ploy. But in fact the Communists had diligently infiltrated Washington. The Democrats were denying evidence and protecting old friends. The most

Opposite: One of the decryptions from Venona. Notice the title-line reference to Enormous — the name the Soviets gave to their all-out campaign to obtain the secrets of the atomic bomb.

The woman in sunglasses on the left is Elizabeth Bentley, known as the Red Spy Queen. Like Chambers, she had been a Communist spy (code-named Umnitsa, meaning "clever girl") but came forward, admitting her crimes and naming others. Here she is speaking to HUAC, while Alger Hiss, who denied all allegations against him until the day he died, sits at the same table, on the far right.

recent count says that from the 1930s until the late 1940s, as many as five hundred Americans were directly assisting the Soviets, and they did real damage. They passed on information about secret weapons, from the atomic bomb to radar and sonar, and did their best to block America from learning Russia's plans.

In what the National Security Agency itself calls "perhaps the most significant intelligence loss in U.S. history," Weisband alone managed to blind our ability to read secret Soviet dispatches just before the Korean War, when Russia was plotting with the North Koreans.

But the anti-Communists were wrong in general—in spreading fear throughout the country, as the Democratic attorney general J. Howard McGrath did in 1950. "There are," he warned, "today many Communists in America. They are everywhere—in factories, offices, butcher stores, on street corners, in private business. And each carries in himself the germ of death for society." With scare words like that, anti-Communists had an easy way to bludgeon union activists, civil rights leaders, intellectuals, and artists.

In turn, the liberals of the time were wrong in specific—in trying to defend the Rosenbergs and the American Communist Party. But they were right in general when, like Senator Smith, they defended the right to dissent. Each side had a partial truth, but that was not clear at the time. Instead, the first five years of the 1950s were truly the Age of Fear.

PART SIX

FACT: After World War II, the Soviets made sure that Communist governments ruled in nearby Europe. Communists were in charge in Hungary, Poland, Czechoslovakia (now the Czech Republic and Slovakia), Romania, Latvia, Lithuania, and Estonia, and in the eastern half of Germany. China had turned Communist, and many of the people seeking to end colonial rule in Africa, Asia, and the Caribbean found inspiration in Communist ideas.

FACT: In 1953, riots broke out in East Germany and spread to some four hundred cities until Soviet tanks restored order. Three years later, a nationwide revolt swept through Hungary, only to be crushed by the Soviets.

The Age of Fear

THE INSIDE STORY: Were the Soviets the allies of common people everywhere, fighting against imperialist nations such as England, France, and America, or were they themselves the worst modern empire builders, crushing free expression anywhere they could? By the mid-'50s, the debates over Stalin and Communism had turned into fights over who would govern throughout the world. And all these clashes were in the shadow of the ever-more-deadly atomic weapons that both America and Russia continued to test by flexing their muscles and showing the death they could spread at the push of a button.

Background photograph: This 1954 film was one of many at the time in which something dark and dangerous welled up from the deep.

LOYALTY

J. Edgar Hoover was content. By all accounts, he was enjoying his "best and happiest years." In 1952, the Republican war hero Dwight D. Eisenhower was elected president with Richard M. Nixon as his vice president. No longer did the director have to battle against an administration that mistrusted him and downplayed the Communist threat. All across America, from nursery schools to government offices, the word was out: be careful, watch what you say, note what you see, guard against the infection of Communism. It is easy to imagine that, now that his fears were shared by the entire nation, Hoover experienced a kind of peace.

In the photo at left, taken in 1953, Hoover is with, from left to right: Senator McCarthy, Clyde Tolson, and the businessman Royal Miller. The four men, with their high pants set at the slopes of their potbellies, standing at the shuffleboard court, look like an advertisement for a senior cruise or an old-time retirement home. You can imagine they play fierce games of pinochle and look forward to a daily shave at the local barbershop. But when

Hoover enjoyed betting on races (especially at the Del Mar track, where there was little risk), being with guys, and rubbing shoulders with celebrities. This card is from the track's founders: singer Bing Crosby, actor Pat O'Brien, and businessman Bill Quigley.

you realize the power Hoover held at just this moment, the photo is chilling. The emotion it conveys is a control so total, it is smug and ugly. In this insulated space there is total safety, complete authority.

The four men are at the Hotel Del Charro, an exclusive resort near San Diego that had strict rules. Jews were almost never allowed in as guests and certainly no blacks, Asians, or Hispanics. The Del Charro was extremely expensive: the bill for Hoover and Tolson's first visit there came to some $20,000 (which would have about the same purchasing power as $163,000 today). But the director never owed a cent. The resort's owner, Clint

Murchison, a fabulously wealthy Texas oilman, reserved Bungalow A just for them and covered their costs.

Everything at the resort needed to be precisely as Hoover wanted it. One time he arrived to find that they did not have his favorite ice cream. FBI agents woke up the man who owned the ice-cream company in the middle of the night, got him to open his plant, then sent a secretary from their office to pick it up and rush it to the waiting director.

Murchison co-owned a nearby racetrack with Sid Richardson, another Texas oil tycoon, and Hoover loved to bet on the horses. But his bets carried no risk. Murchison gave him inside tips. It was the same with oil drilling. Most people who invest in an oil well are taking a big gamble; if the well comes up dry, they lose. But Murchison told Hoover where to invest, and he did not collect if a well failed. Hoover was insulated by the limitless Murchison fortune, just as he was protected by the new administration. He lived on an island of wealth and power cordoned off from the concerns of blacks, Jews, union organizers, and social critics.

Hoover at the Del Charro with his wealthy Texas oilmen hosts

Almost all the African Americans he worked with—even if they were officially FBI agents—acted as his domestic help, driving his car, grooming his garden, or cleaning his house. The Jews he knew were allies in anti-Communism (such as McCarthy's aide Roy Cohn) and/or wealthy themselves (such as the liquor magnate Lewis Rosenstiel). Hoover was clean, successful, and supremely powerful. And then there was McCarthy, just at the edge, ready to go back out into the world, to do the dirty work.

During the visit to the Del Charro, Hoover gave an interview with a local newspaper and spoke appreciatively about McCarthy: He "is a former Marine. He was an amateur boxer. He's Irish. Combine those, and you're going to have a vigorous individual, who is not going to be pushed around. . . . I view him as a friend and believe he so views me." McCarthy was the man's man who would "attack subversives" and take heat for it. "But," Hoover added, using the formula that defined his own life, "sometimes a knock is a boost." McCarthy was the young tough who was going to swing away at the nation's enemies while his proud godfather watched from within his gated compound.

Murchison had been one of the secret sponsors when McCarthy used a fake photo against Tydings. H. L. Hunt, another very wealthy Texas oilman, paid for radio and television shows that spread the message of extreme anti-Communism. The Hunt broadcasts were explicitly anti-Semitic and racist—one program defended slavery in America as "benign" compared to "barbaric" practices in Africa. That was the outer fringe of the anti-Communist movement. With McCarthy leading the way, a chill edge of fear influenced the entire nation. The Smith Act of 1940 had made it illegal for Communists to speak about revolution, even if there was no evidence that they were plotting any action. By 1954, 52 percent of Americans felt that all Communists should be put in prison, while an astonishing 80 percent believed Communists should lose their citizenship.

There was no room in the law anymore for John Reed, or Paul Robeson, or the angry Richard Wright. In a strict sense, Communist ideas were legal, but Communist Party leaders were convicted criminals. People who owned copies of books by Marx and Lenin began to cover them with brown paper

Hoover and Tolson, probably in 1952—their clothing is similar but no longer identical. They could be any bureaucrats working in any business at the time. In fact, a best-selling novel about businessmen of the day was called The Man in the Gray Flannel Suit*—though the man in the book had his own wartime secret to hide. There was something both reassuring and unsettling about the pressure to conform.*

and hide them on their shelves. This was no idle fear. Indeed, in one case, a government employee was considered unreliable because "you maintained in your library books on Communism, Socialism, and Marxism."

Hoover no longer gallivanted around with Tolson in eye-catching white suits and expensive leather shoes. Though they still sometimes wore similar suit jackets, the colors were gray, the styling conventional. They were meant to look just like every other office manager. Hoover treasured conformity in thought, in belief, in appearance, in action. He wanted people to behave like orderly notes on file cards. Mark Felt had already been an FBI agent for twelve years when, in 1954, he was invited to meet Hoover. He knew he needed careful instruction in exactly how to perform. His "handshake had to be firm but not too firm. Hoover disliked a 'bone crusher' as well as a limp grip. He detested moist palms, and we were told to have a dry handkerchief ready to wipe off any sweat before the crucial handclasp."

Felt noticed Hoover's "immaculate appearance"; then—and always—he seemed in "complete control." The director expected exactly the same discipline and self-control from his men. His agents all wore the same white shirts and dark suits and socks and had the same short, neatly cut hair. Like a fanatical schoolteacher, Hoover insisted that FBI memos have precisely the same amount of white space in their borders. Indeed, in order to make sure he was not being followed, Hoover ruled that all his car trips must be mapped out with only right turns.

The fact that Hoover's dress code made FBI agents easy to spot did not seem to concern him. He needed the public to see the FBI as the perfect image of order and discipline. That way, he believed, citizens would turn over information to the Bureau — and hesitate to commit crimes. But of course the standard dress made life much easier for the Soviets. A one-time Communist spy later wrote that it was all too easy to spot G-men, with "their clothing style, guilty-thievish glances, and clumsy manners."

Hoover's agency of well-trained conformists played a key part in the effort to root anything smacking of Communism out of American life. But the FBI was hardly alone. Eager anti-Communists could be found everywhere, from the smallest town to the largest city. The Bureau echoed, as much as it created, the national mood of fear. By the early 1950s, the loyalty oath system that President Truman had established spread far and wide, and the need to check on a person's beliefs gave the FBI a perfect excuse to pry into private lives. By 1955, about one in every five American workers was required to take an oath swearing that he or she was not a Communist and was "loyal" to the United States.

How could you spot a Communist? It was as if the whole country were living in the lines of Hoover's file system—noting down anything strange, anything unusual, anything out of the ordinary. A housewife in Oregon suspected a neighbor of being a Communist because "he was always talking about world peace." A railroad worker in Michigan caught a hint of danger when he "saw a map of Russia" hanging on a wall in a nearby house. A woman in San Francisco reported a fellow employee because "he would never wear his tie home or his coat home. . . . For a while he wore one of those great big mustaches and I have heard people say that . . . those are indications that he is not a capitalist."

While busybody neighbors reported on maps and ties, officers of the law found new reasons for suspicion. When the American tanks rolled into Holland at the end of World War II, Trude Guermonprez (my aunt) was starving. She saw her first American soldiers while out in a field digging up tulip bulbs to feed herself. Though she was Jewish, she managed to evade the Nazis throughout the war, while her husband, a gentile, had been one of the leaders of the Dutch Resistance. He was captured and executed by the Nazis, and in honor of his heroism, the postwar Dutch government offered to support her. But she chose to join her parents, who were teaching at a college in America. When the anti-Communist crusade began in earnest, several government men called on the college and argued that Trude should not be allowed to stay in the country. The fact that her husband had been in the Dutch Resistance suggested to them that he might have been a Communist. That was how wide the blanket of fear spread: having fought against the genocidal Nazis implied being a nonconformist, a person opposed to authority, a rebel, perhaps a red. The college stood up for my aunt, who went on to become an American citizen. But most of those who came under suspicion were not as lucky.

The author Howard Fast was a public member of the Communist Party, and the FBI continually buzzed around him. He and his wife, Bette, were

Opposite: In ethnic urban neighborhoods, Catholic teenagers fueled by anti-Communist fire clashed with Jewish young people marching for leftist causes. The Cold War between America and the Soviet Union was also fought on city streets.

followed on the streets, their phones were tapped, and a babysitter hired to watch their children tried to place electronic bugs in their house. In 1950, he was sentenced to three months in prison for refusing to cooperate with HUAC. While he was away, his wife later told their daughter, Rachel, only one person called to check in on the family. "They were afraid. Everyone was afraid." Old friends walked by the Fast family in restaurants and pretended not to see them. "There were agents watching, everywhere," Bette Fast recalled, "noting who knew whom, who talked to whom. We understood it. You can't image how it was. It was a terrible time. Terrible."

In the 1930s, the Chicago Communists threw Richard Wright out of a May Day parade and marched past him with blank faces. In 1950, people were so afraid of being seen as Communists that they averted their eyes from the Fast family. The flags had changed, but the pressure to conform was just as strong.

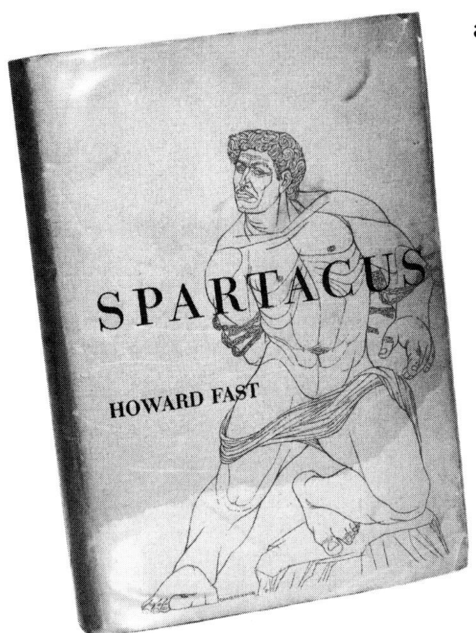

The original cover of Howard Fast's Spartacus

Fast decided to use his skill as a writer to deal with his jailing. But he did not write a memoir. Instead, he wrote a novel about Spartacus, the gladiator-slave who led a massive revolt in Rome in 73 BCE. Spartacus was a great hero to many on the left, from Marx on, because he seemed to be an early, strong example of the downtrodden fighting back and battling to take control of society.

The first editor to read Fast's book was Angus Cameron, then vice president and editor in chief at Little, Brown, a major publishing house. Cameron loved it. But, as he later told Fast, "J. Edgar Hoover had sent his personal emissary, a federal agent, to Boston, where he met with the president of Little, Brown. He told him that he was not to publish any more books by Howard Fast, that those were the express instructions of J. Edgar Hoover." Even though Fast was a popular author who had been publishing for twenty years, not one publisher would take his book. He had to publish it himself.

The book sold nearly fifty thousand copies in hardcover, but, Fast later said, when a major paperback house printed another hundred thousand, the FBI insisted that the publisher destroy the copies. Fast had to buy them and sell them himself.

One government official who tested employees to see if they had any dangerous ideas revealed a telltale sign: “Of course the fact that a person believes in racial equality doesn’t *prove* that he’s a Communist, but it certainly makes you look twice, doesn’t it?” A witness in another loyalty case used the same standard: “My impression was that he thought the colored should be entitled to as much as anybody else, and naturally I differed on that.” Speaking up for equality and, worse, integration did make FBI men and loyalty board officers “look twice.” The army made that explicit when it published a helpful guide titled *How to Spot a Communist.* Keen observers were told to keep an eye out for people who talked about civil rights, or discrimination, or anti-union legislation.

By 1953, the purifiers were not satisfied with the loyalty system, because too many people were being cleared. So the standard for working in government was tightened; in addition to loyalty oaths, there were now staff clearances. Now you could be fired for whom you might love, not just for a cause you once supported or a petition you signed twenty years earlier. If it was rumored that you were homosexual, for example, you could be let go as a “security risk.” The government did not have to prove that you were a homosexual or that enemy agents were actually blackmailing you. Security officers claimed they needed to fire employees if a lie detector test showed that they had kissed, desired, or had fantasies about someone of the same sex at any point in their lives. Of the 654 people who were forced to leave the State Department between 1947 and 1953, during the height of the Age of Fear, 402 were alleged or suspected to have been homosexual.

This entire program of prying and suspicion was based on a false premise. There was not a single proven instance in which a person was coerced into giving up secrets to the Soviets because of his or her homosexual orientation. Not one. In fact, it was Washington politicians’ many heterosexual affairs that filled blackmailers’ files. Still, the head of the State Department’s

Bureau of Security insisted that the firing of suspected homosexuals must continue. "There can be no proof, since future events are not susceptible to proof." (For a film that captures the effect of the homosexual fear on Washington, see *Advise and Consent,* the first Hollywood feature film to deal with homosexuality.)

PURGE

The FBI was not the only organization interested in who attended a May Day rally or came to pay respects at the funeral of old Communist Party members. Hoover's elaborate file system was echoed by anti-Communist watchdog groups, which claimed to be combining a public service with good business. The American Security Council (ASC), for example, employed ex–FBI agents to piece together a list of some one million supposedly radical Americans, which it then offered for sale to concerned employers. The lists did not have to be perfect; organizations like ASC were not holding trials with rules of evidence. They merely made available the names of Americans they had reason to suspect. But since the company itself decided on the criteria for suspicion, criminals saw a golden opportunity. On some of these lists, if you saw your name, you could pay a fee to be "cleared." Blackmailers learned to play a similar game with charges of homosexuality. They would stage a seemingly compromising encounter between one of their team and an unsuspecting man, then offer to keep quiet for a price.

In the early 1950s, the actual threat of Soviet spying was declining due to the Venona decryptions and because American Communists were losing their faith. Party leaders had scattered to avoid being put in jail, and the Party was making impossible demands on those who were left. By 1954, Howard Fast felt that "much as the FBI was destroying the party, the party was destroying itself." But even as the number of real Communists in America plummeted, a toxic atmosphere spread throughout the country. All of Washington feared Hoover's files. And mini-Hoovers around the country held the same power locally. Conservatives claimed that both the United States government and United Nations were filled with unmanly pencil

Ten Hollywood writers, producers, and directors, including the screenwriter Dalton Trumbo, refused to answer HUAC's questions about their Communist pasts and were sent to prison for contempt of Congress. Afterward, they were blacklisted—unable to get work in Hollywood, at least at their old pay rates and under their real names. Trumbo moved to Mexico.

pushers whose only loyalty was to the global homosexual Soviet underground. Out in Hollywood, Myron Fagan claimed that a secret society sponsored by Jews was conspiring to use the UN to take over the world and that famous film stars were pawns in this dastardly plot. Suspicion became proof.

The glamorous Hollywood studios, with their he-men and curvaceous babes, were particularly vulnerable to whispers of disloyalty. Then, as now, there was a ready market for gossip about movie stars. And gossip columnists were as ready to spread suspicion, or employ blackmail, as anyone else. So there was a constant bubble of accusation and fear made all the worse because the major studios were seeing their profits decline. TV was the new sensation, and people were choosing to stay home with their families rather than go out to the movies. Hollywood simply could not tolerate bad

A woman who had sat across from Hoover once wrote that "his look of supreme confidence—can confidence be evil?—was absolutely frightening," In this 1952 photo, you can see that complete and immobile certainty. The world was under his control and as he liked it.

publicity. In 1951, when HUAC decided to hold hearings about Communists in the film world, everyone knew the score. You would say or do whatever the committee wanted, or your film career was over.

The committee already knew a great deal about who was, or had once been, a Communist. The hearings were not really meant to gather new information. Rather, committee members wanted suspects to grovel. Each witness was asked to spill the names of friends, neighbors, and lovers to demonstrate his or her own loyalty by betraying others. It didn't even matter if everyone a person named had already been identified as a former Communist or Communist sympathizer. The goal was to force people to vomit out the past, to expel it like a disease. A witness who had once been a leftist now needed to show that he or she had no old alliance, no lingering bond of friendship, no emotion at all but obedience to the committee.

The HUAC hearings and the whole loyalty campaign were the judgment of the 1950s on the 1930s. In the 1930s, you may have thought you were being idealistic in speaking up for the Scottsboro Nine, sending money to support widows overseas, or buying a Paul Robeson record. You may have seen yourself as a patriotic American, bringing Jefferson's ideals to the twentieth century. But twenty years later, you learned that you had been terribly wrong. Those who had disagreed with you during the Depression, or who might need to cover up their own youthful radicalism by exposing yours, were going to make you pay.

The poet Langston Hughes testifying before HUAC in 1953. Radicalized by the Scottsboro trials, he had traveled to the Soviet Union to make a movie designed to bring the Communist message to African Americans. But by the 1950s, he had abandoned those beliefs. He did his best to please the committee without having to harm anyone else.

Actor Larry Parks experienced the mood of the committee in 1951. He was ready to admit that he had once been a member of the Communist Party. But that was not enough for his examiners. "Don't present me with the choice of either being in contempt of this committee and going to jail," he pleaded, "or forcing me to really crawl through the mud to be an informer." But that is precisely what HUAC demanded. Parks tried to push back: "It seems to me that this is not the American way of doing things. . . . I think to do something like this is more akin to what happened under Hitler, and what is happening in Russia today. . . . It is not befitting for this committee to force me to make this kind of choice." But the committee did want Parks to choose—betray your friends, ruin their careers for having once shared the wrong ideals, or get out of Hollywood. Parks finally did name names—and still got only two more parts for the rest of the decade.

The price of refusing to give names was even higher. J. Edward Bromberg was an actor, but when HUAC called on him, he would not cooperate. His son Conrad later recalled the weeks, months, and years that followed: "I remember a sense of silence that pervaded that apartment. . . . Very few people came to see us. . . . He would be sitting at his desk waiting for the phone to ring. . . . He would literally sit for hours and hours." Two years after he met the committee and his phone stopped ringing, Bromberg died; he was forty-eight years old.

Theater artists cannot stand silence. Stranded on a desert island with a few tools, a painter can still paint, an author can write. But a director needs actors, and actors crave an audience. We call the most famous people in Hollywood "stars" because they blaze—they give off heat and light. Being cut off from the flow of energy—not to speak of the fame and fortune it brings—is terrifying. The biggest spirit may be in the most danger; he who has the most to give has the most to lose. Take Elia Kazan.

Kazan was a brilliant director. Even today, if you watch the Oscar-winning films he made, such as *Gentleman's Agreement* or *On the Waterfront,* you can feel the sharp intelligence and burning intensity he brought to a project. As a young man in the 1930s, Kazan joined the distinctly left-wing Group Theater (as did my father), and for a couple of years he was a member of a secret Communist cell (my father was not tempted). As a result, on January 14, 1952, Kazan was called to face HUAC.

In Elia Kazan's film On the Waterfront, *the heroic individual stands up by breaking ranks with the corrupt union. In Arthur Miller's play* The Crucible, *the heroic individual resists the impulse to save himself by accusing others. In these works, the two former friends, Kazan and Miller, were both talking about HUAC, Communism, and anti-Communism—from opposite points of view.*

Kazan knew how to read a scene—he staged them all the time. He felt how much the congressmen enjoyed their power and his helplessness. And he was sure the committee already knew everything it needed to know about him and the Group Theater. Their real goal was to conduct "a degradation ceremony," in which he had to kneel and inform on his friends. He refused to speak about anyone but himself. But Kazan had seen the Communists play the same power games. He remembered hearing writers being told how to write and his own fear of disagreeing. He had let "the Party fellows get away with what I hated most, by not being ready to question and doubt and forcefully express my contrary convictions." And he knew for certain that he could direct films again only if he agreed to name names. To speak was to give in and hurt his friends. But the alternative was that killing silence—silence about the Communists he disliked and the silence of a career cut short.

Kazan's side of this story is best explained by watching *On the Waterfront,* a film written by Budd Schulberg, who freely spoke to HUAC, starring Lee J. Cobb, who also named names, and directed by Kazan. It is about an individual who is brave enough to expose corruption and tell the truth to the police. The hero is the man who resists the group and speaks for himself.

In his own mind, Kazan made the right choice. He named eight people, all actual Communists; he was telling the truth. But the truth bears a price. Philip Loeb was starring in a TV series about a Jewish family called *The Goldbergs.* When Kazan and Cobb both named him as having once been a Communist, he was taken off the TV series and could not find work. In 1955, Loeb committed suicide. Like J. Edward Bromberg, he could not take the silence.

When Kazan first started working on a movie about the waterfront, his scriptwriter was the playwright Arthur Miller. Miller and Kazan were a terrific creative team; they were also friends and lived near each other in Connecticut. In the early days of 1952, as Kazan was deciding what to say to HUAC, Miller stopped by his house. He was on his way to research a new play about the Salem witch trials of 1692. While Kazan was unsure what to say to the committee, Miller had no doubts. Called before HUAC, Miller insisted that "I could not use the name of another person and bring trouble on him." His play about Salem was to be a comment on the modern witch hunt going on in America.

Miller arrived at his friend's house, then realized something was wrong: Kazan had already broken, given the committee what it wanted. Miller was furious—at HUAC. "I was," he later wrote, "experiencing a bitterness with the country that I had never even imagined before, a hatred of its stupidity and its throwing away of its freedom. Who or what was safer now because this man in his human weakness had been forced to humiliate himself?" You can still feel Miller's fury when you see the play he went on to write, *The Crucible.*

NO DECENCY

Joe McCarthy rose to power by bullying everyone, going beyond all limits. But he was just as out of control in his personal life. By 1954, he was drinking too much, eating too much, and talking too much. He was like a guy at a party whom people enjoy at first for being rude and crude but who goes too far. There is a moment when even his fans turn away, when what was entertaining turns scary or sad. One night at the Del Charro, McCarthy was so drunk that he angrily pushed his nicely dressed new bride into a pool. Murchison got up, walked away, and sent a note to McCarthy telling him to leave the hotel.

On March 9, Edward R. Murrow, the most trusted reporter on television, devoted a full half-hour show to challenging the "situation of fear" McCarthy was spreading. Calls to the network ran 10–1 in favor of the show and against McCarthy. (The 2005 film *Good Night, and Good Luck* recounts this story.)

McCarthy's boorish behavior was the least of his worries. One of his aides had tried to coerce the army into giving him special treatment. When the

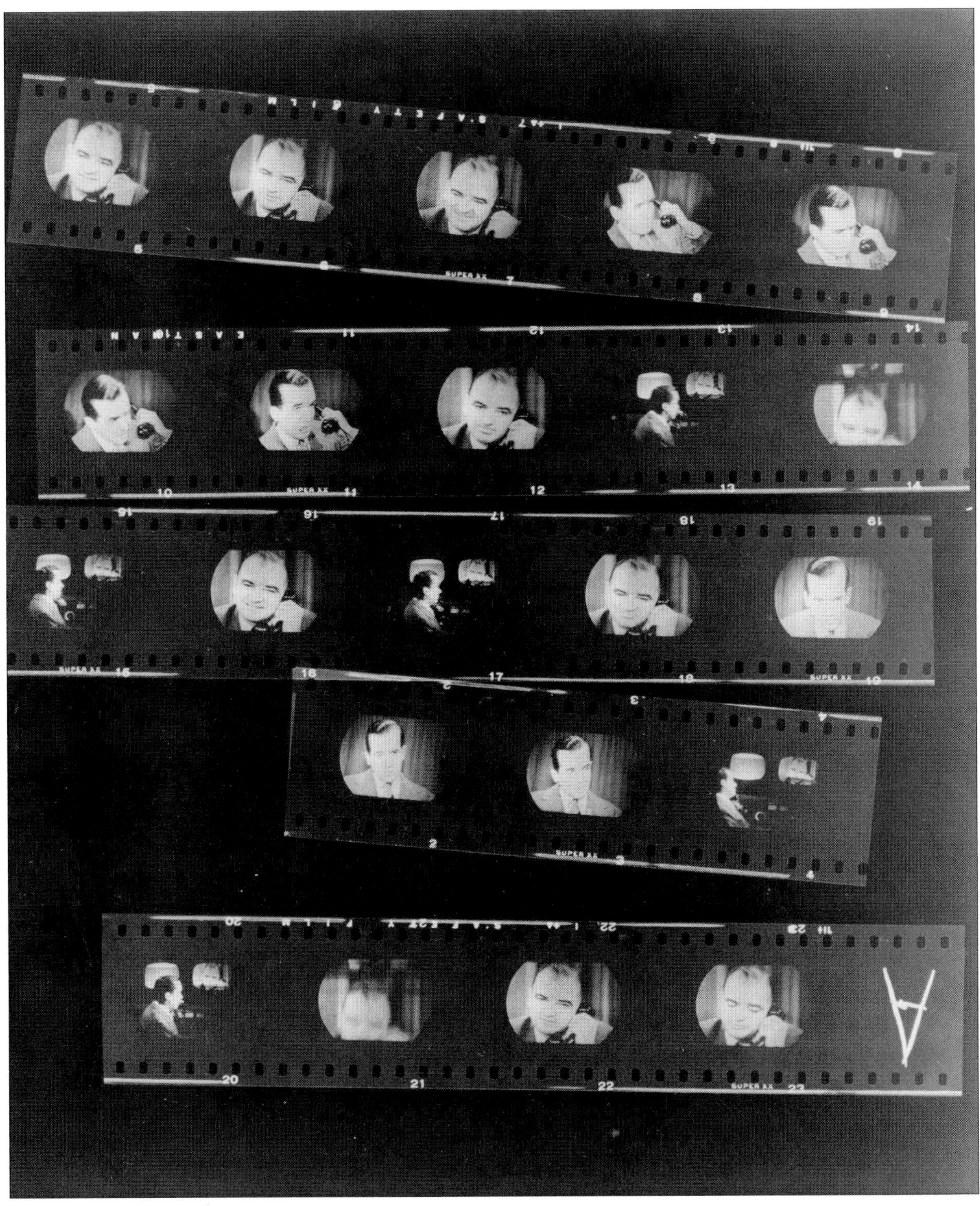
5 6 SUPER XX 7 8 9
10 SUPER XX 11 12 13 14
SUPER XX 15 16 17 18 SUPER XX 19
2 SUPER XX 3 4
20 21 22 SUPER XX 23

military balked, McCarthy accused the soldiers of hiding traitors. McCarthy was about to challenge the army—in a nation where many were proud of their service and the memories of recent wars burned bright. He did not know it, but he was going to have to do it alone.

McCarthy was so out of control, he made the one mistake Hoover could not forgive: he brought suspicion on the FBI. The senator was making it too easy for people to guess where he was getting his information, and Hoover would never, ever, allow his Bureau to look bad. The director ordered his men to cut him loose—no more lists, no names, no more favors. Just when McCarthy took on the army, he lost his secret support system. All he had left was his bluster and his nearly limitless capacity for cruelty.

The Army-McCarthy hearings began on April 22, 1954, and lasted until June 17. Two television networks covered every moment of the drama. The attorney for the army was an old-time Boston lawyer named Joseph Welch. One day when Welch was questioning Roy Cohn, McCarthy's closest aide, McCarthy broke in. He accused Welch of having an assistant who was himself a Communist. In fact, the assistant had once supported a liberal lawyers' group—a cause of suspicion in the Age of Fear but certainly no proof of being a traitor. "Until this moment, Senator," Welch responded, his face heavy with feeling, "I think I never really gauged your cruelty or your recklessness." McCarthy *was* being reckless, lashing out at Welch, at the army, at anyone and everyone he could name. As film cameras rolled, Welch captured the worst of McCarthy—the bully who would rather hurt others than show weakness. "Let us not assassinate this lad further, Senator. You have done enough. Have you no sense of decency, sir, at long last? Have you left no sense of decency?" (The 1964 documentary *Point of Order* tells this story very well.)

McCarthy couldn't sleep; he drank at breakfast and at lunch and seemed on the edge of collapse. But he tried to rally support by playing on his old themes. Twenty-five thousand Communists, he warned, were spread across America, ready to support the U.S.S.R. "They know exactly where to throw a

Opposite: Edward R. Murrow interviewing Senator McCarthy in a national broadcast

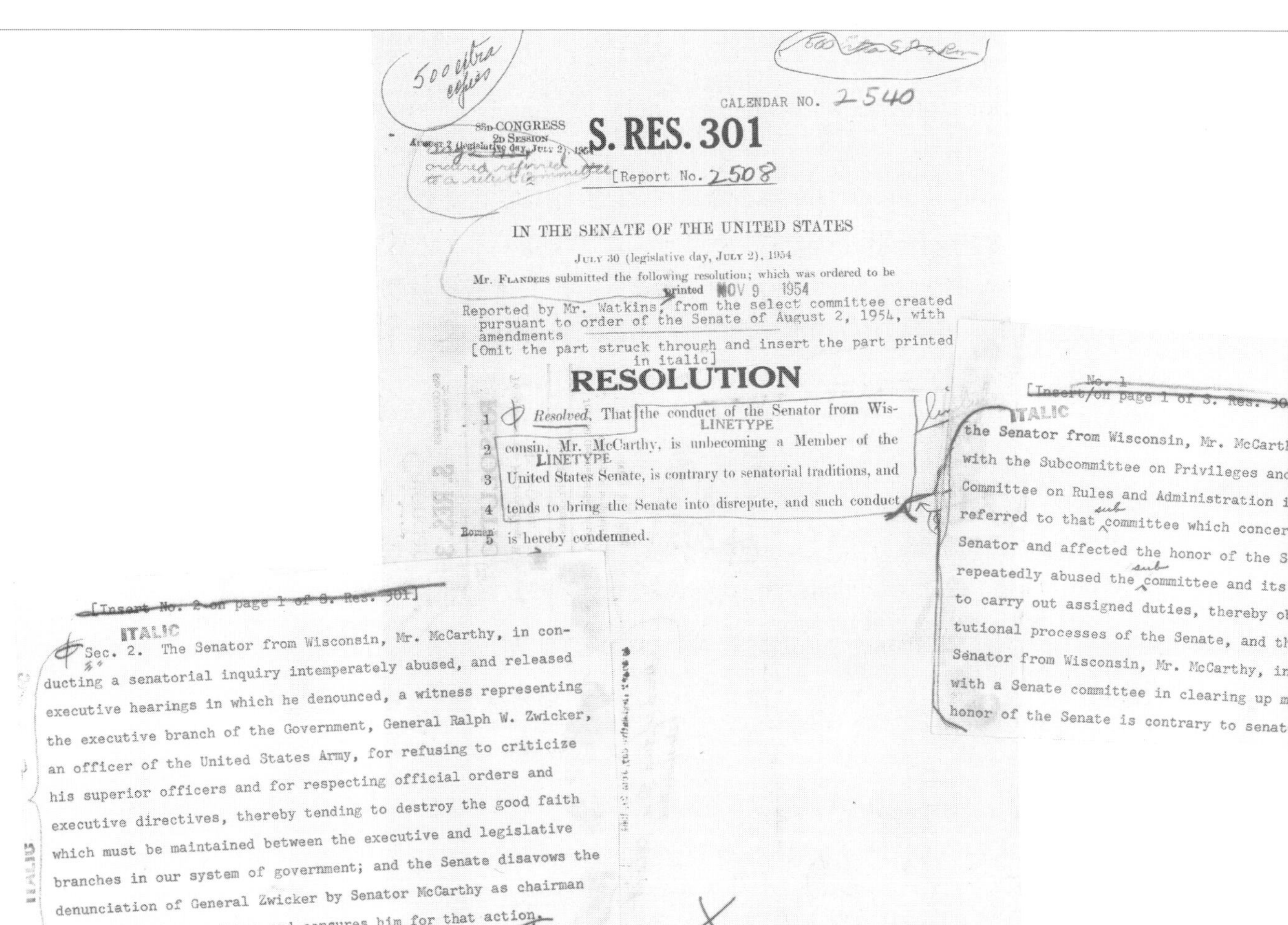

500 extra copies

CALENDAR NO. 2540

83D CONGRESS
2D SESSION

S. RES. 301

[Report No. 2508]

IN THE SENATE OF THE UNITED STATES

JULY 30 (legislative day, JULY 2), 1954

Mr. FLANDERS submitted the following resolution; which was ordered to be printed NOV 9 1954

Reported by Mr. Watkins, from the select committee created pursuant to order of the Senate of August 2, 1954, with amendments

[Omit the part struck through and insert the part printed in italic]

RESOLUTION

1 *Resolved*, That the conduct of the Senator from Wis-
2 consin, Mr. McCarthy, is unbecoming a Member of the
3 United States Senate, is contrary to senatorial traditions, and
4 tends to bring the Senate into disrepute, and such conduct
5 is hereby condemned.

[Insert No. 2 on page 1 of S. Res. 301]

ITALIC

Sec. 2. The Senator from Wisconsin, Mr. McCarthy, in conducting a senatorial inquiry intemperately abused, and released executive hearings in which he denounced, a witness representing the executive branch of the Government, General Ralph W. Zwicker, an officer of the United States Army, for refusing to criticize his superior officers and for respecting official orders and executive directives, thereby tending to destroy the good faith which must be maintained between the executive and legislative branches in our system of government; and the Senate disavows the denunciation of General Zwicker by Senator McCarthy as chairman of a Senate subcommittee and censures him for that action.

No. 1
[Insert on page 1 of S. Res. 301]

ITALIC

the Senator from Wisconsin, Mr. McCarth
with the Subcommittee on Privileges and
Committee on Rules and Administration i
referred to that subcommittee which concer
Senator and affected the honor of the Se
repeatedly abused the subcommittee and its
to carry out assigned duties, thereby ob
tutional processes of the Senate, and th
Senator from Wisconsin, Mr. McCarthy, in
with a Senate committee in clearing up m
honor of the Senate is contrary to senat

A draft of the Senate resolution condemning Senator McCarthy. From the moment he made his FBI connection too obvious, his days were numbered. Without Hoover's support, his bullying lost its power.

long chain or a steel cable to cut off the electric power of any city in case of war with Russia. . . . They teach goon squads how to throw hand grenades, how in effect to commit murder." Mitchell Palmer had issued similar warnings as his popularity declined. For years after the September 11, 2001, attacks, Fox News ran alert levels on its TV crawlers, reminding everyone to be scared, to be afraid. But there is a moment when stirring up fear no longer works. It only makes the fearmonger look desperate. In January 1954, half of Americans polled said they liked McCarthy. By June, when he was shamed by Welch, only 34 percent were still on his side, while 45 percent disliked him. By December, the Senate censured McCarthy, and his days of power were over.

Reporters next turned their attention to the people who had supported McCarthy, men like H. L. Hunt and Clint Murchison. Exposés spoke of Texas as a state dominated by "hate, fear, and suspicion" whipped up by "a handful of prodigiously wealthy men." Instead of defining patriotic Americanism, Texas money seemed toxic.

Hoover was not tainted. He had used McCarthy as a front man but knew exactly when to step away. Two years after his censure, in 1956, Joe McCarthy was an obvious alcoholic, liquor dribbling out of his mouth as he downed shot after shot. He died the next year. Hoover, with his files, his secrets, and his G-men, was alive and well, but he had a problem of his own. The mood in the country was shifting, and that shift would lead him into his last battle.

PART SEVEN

FACT: While Hoover was head of the FBI, President Kennedy was assassinated, as were Dr. King, Senator Robert Kennedy, Malcolm X, and the Black Panther leader Fred Hampton. The Internet is filled with conspiracy theories claiming that Hoover and the FBI either plotted these murders or did little to prevent them.

THE INSIDE STORY: The FBI had information about Kennedy's assassin, Lee Harvey Oswald, that should have led it to pay more attention to him. They were inept, and Hoover did his best to cover that up. But that was not the Bureau at its worst. A recent biography of Malcolm X that makes extensive use of FBI files concludes that agents had infiltrated his inner circle but were strangely absent when he was killed. There is so much evidence that agents were involved in Hampton's death that the FBI agreed to pay a million dollars into a fund set up in his name. It is, though, unfair to expect any agency to have provided perfect security in a period when America was in deep conflict with itself and when many groups and individuals believed in violent revolution. The FBI's failures both deepened and reflected the intense divisions of the time.

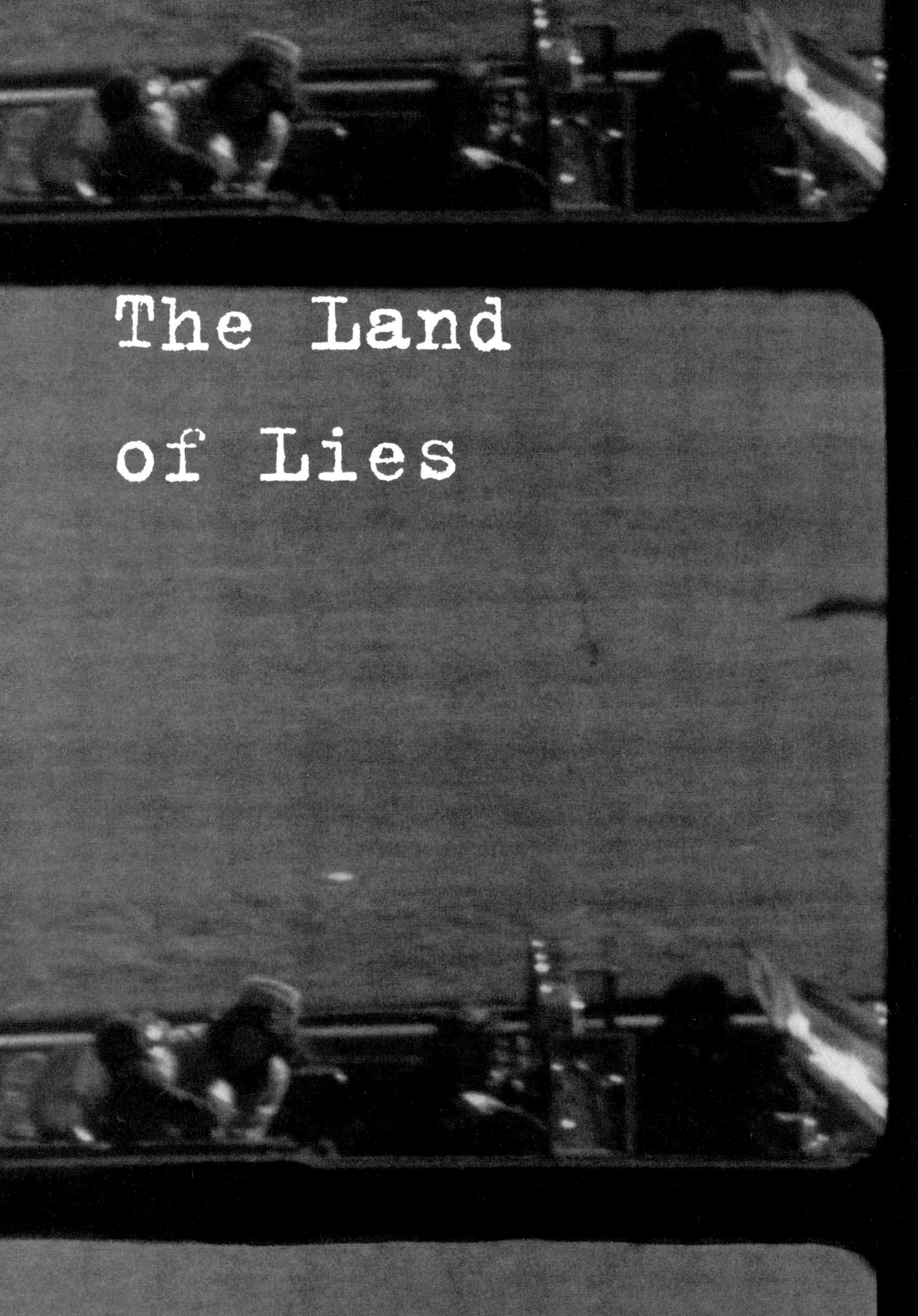

The Land of Lies

Background photograph: Frames from the twenty-six-second film Abraham Zapruder recorded on November 22, 1963. He had planned to film the president's visit to Dallas but instead captured Kennedy's assassination.

The 1954 Supreme Court decision in Brown v. Board of Education of Topeka signaled trouble for Hoover. The highest court in the land announced that the policies of separation and conformity he had devoted his life to defending were illegal. While junior and senior high schools took longer to integrate, elementary classrooms, such as the previously all-white Barnard School, in Washington, DC, shown here in 1955, were quick to implement change.

16 THE SPECTER

J. Edgar Hoover grew from each of his battles. By chasing down gangsters and then broadcasting that story through the mass media, he made himself a national hero. When "subversives" threatened America, he met with the president in secret to map out a response. After FDR's death, he turned his own recollection of the private meeting into a mandate to vastly extend the Bureau's secret reach. From that moment on, Hoover's career as a lawman meshed perfectly with his private fears. The FBI was built on Hoover's passion for scientific precision, careful management, and secrecy. But starting in the mid-1950s, if he was going to follow orders and enforce the law, he was going to have to turn against his own deepest beliefs and prejudices. The two foundations of his entire being—protecting himself and protecting his nation—were about to come into conflict. The first hint of this new threat came from the Supreme Court in 1954, when it ruled that all public schools must be integrated. This meant trouble for Hoover and the FBI.

Hoover was a Washington man through and through. He fought hard each year to get more money from Congress, to gain new responsibilities for the FBI. Yet his idea was always that elite FBI agents would work with local police forces. His FBI was to be a model that police chiefs, mayors, and American Legionnaires would so admire that they would serve as its loyal friends and allies. To enforce racial integration in the South would mean having to clash with, overrule, and even arrest the very people he counted on for support. Nothing about that prospect appealed to Hoover.

How could he, Hoover asked with absolute puzzlement, expect his men to enforce orders that required southern cops to stop saying "Boy, come here" and instead address black men as "Mr."? The very idea seemed ludicrous to him. Hoover loved coming to Congress and showing off the FBI's astonishing and ever-improving record of success—how many crimes it had solved, how often cases it brought resulted in convictions. If the FBI started to bring white people accused of resisting integration before the largely white southern juries they would surely face, his conviction rate would plummet. Instead of being seen as an elite authority, the FBI would come across as both alien and ineffectual. He hated that thought. But Hoover was ultimately a Washington bureaucrat. His men would follow orders. After 1944, when

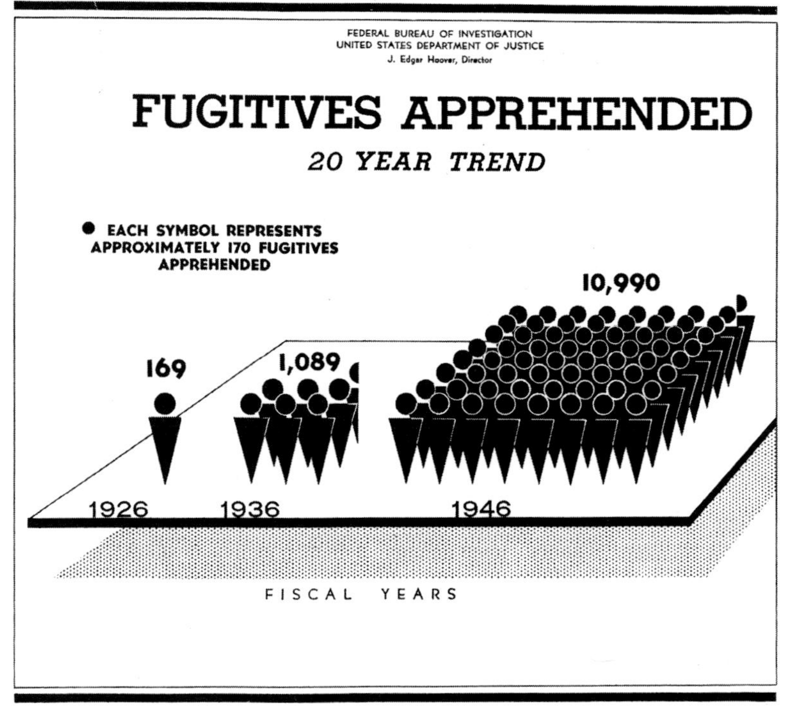

the Supreme Court overruled all-white primary elections in the South, FBI agents were assigned to investigate voting rights cases. Indeed, pressed by a black congressman, Hoover began to make sure that more of his agents in the South were northerners so that, at least on paper, they would have some distance from local attitudes.

Hoover always did what he was required to do. But his resistance to the struggle for black rights runs like a thread through his entire life, from his campaign against Marcus Garvey to his obsession with the Communist Party role in the Scottsboro defense. There was something about the move toward integration that shook him on an emotional level, below thought. Analyzing southern white resistance to integration, he said that "colored parents are not as careful in looking after the health and cleanliness of their children." And those parents might well be living immoral lives, having children without being married. Thus the fear haunting whites was "the specter of racial intermarriage."

Hoover's world had always been neatly divided into the categories his mother had taught him: law and lawlessness, purity and immorality, and as he grew up, he folded Christian America and Communist Russia into the pattern. He often said that Communism itself was not the problem, as it was merely "the latest form of the eternal rebellion against authority." If blacks were not kept down, they would rise up and flood the white world of law, morals, and faithful marriage. Black Americans were like the beast inside Hoover himself, which he said would be let loose if he ever loved a woman and she betrayed him. If he had grown up in a home haunted by the "specter" of its own African-American ancestry, the question of black rights was not one of law but of his own essence. Something was rising in the country—something strange, large, and terrifying—and it was threatening the walls of Hoover's carefully constructed world.

In 1954, the FBI was not required to take an active role in monitoring the civil rights struggle. None of the branches of government—executive,

Opposite: Hoover was masterful at preparing such charts to demonstrate the FBI's ever-greater success. If the FBI were to clash with segregationists and their supporters in the South, it would only ensure a decline in federal arrests and convictions.

THE MAN WHO INVENTED GOSSIP

THE END

Josephine Baker was an African-American singer and dancer who was better known and more popular in France than in America. She was a true international star and a visible, outspoken opponent of racial segregation. On October 16, 1951, she came to the place any celebrity would visit in New York: the Stork Club. Just then one of the biggest hits on Broadway was the musical *South Pacific,* which took its own pathbreaking stand against racism in both its storyline and its popular songs. Baker was accompanied to the club by a group that included Roger Rico, a French singer who was one of the leading men in the show. They arrived after eleven p.m., normal enough for a club that served stars after they finished their performances. But she got the distinct impression that she was not welcome. The club's owner, Sherman Billingsley, had built his reputation on recognizing his guests and anticipating their needs. He ignored her, and for an hour Baker's party watched waiters whiz by—without ever being

Jo Baker

Jo Baker Snubbed At Stork Club

Josephine Baker, international stage star, who only recently was voted "the world's best dressed woman" in an unofficial poll on the Stork Club's TV show, this week was planning legal ac-

served. Baker claimed that Walter Winchell was seated nearby and seemed equally determined to pretend she was not there.

Baker and the NAACP sued the club for discrimination, and Winchell became the object of a barrage of criticism. He was Mr. Stork Club, as well as the voice of the nation. Shouldn't he stand up for Baker, for integration, for principle? Winchell did just the opposite. Angry at being criticized, he became increasingly outraged at Baker, at the NAACP, and at the causes they supported. Winchell, like Hoover, chose to fight for the world he knew, not the world that was taking shape. He became more and more a difficult, even obnoxious, figure of the past. Though he continued to write his column, speak on radio, and even occasionally host a TV show, he seemed bitter, dated, and out of step with his times. (For a brilliant portrait of the worst of Winchell—based on reality but with some fictional touches—see the movie *The Sweet Smell of Success*.)

was told abruptly that "a search" was being made for the shrimp cocktail and steak she had ordered.

Embarrassed at being inten-

Jo

legislative, or judicial—was eager to tangle with segregation, so Hoover's reluctance was fully within the law. And yet, when Hoover felt it was right for his Bureau to act, he found his own way around the rules. And the change in the national mood was not just in the area of civil rights.

Three years after overturning segregation in schools, the Supreme Court made a second decision that challenged Hoover's world. In 1957, the court ruled against the idea that Communist Party members could be jailed for merely believing in revolution. Though World War II was long over, Hoover had kept up and modified his secret list of people to sweep away and hold in "custodial detention." The Security Index, now termed the Registry List, was his latest plan for protection by separation: knowing whom to jail in order to keep the rest of America safe.

FBI leaders gathered and decided that if they could no longer arrest Party members based on their beliefs, they would have to do something new. Instead of spying on revolutionaries, the director would pay informers to enter Communist cells and secret meetings and sow dissention from within. For forty years, FBI men had gathered intelligence. In 1956, they began a Counter-Intelligence Program, COINTELPRO. COINTELPRO was Hoover's triumph and his final fall.

TRIUMPH

In 1956, Nikita Khrushchev, the new head of the Soviet Union, gave a speech in which he detailed Stalin's crimes. When Howard Fast read a translation of those "twenty thousand words of horror and infamy," he "exploded with rage." Fast was finally realizing that he had devoted his life, risked his family, to protect a lie.

Hoover saw that the American Communist Party was teetering, so he set out to push it over. Paid informers signed up to join the Party, then angrily brought up Stalin's murders. They caused rifts between factions, further splintering the tiny organization. In order to weaken a Party member, people working for the Bureau would "dress him in a snitch jacket"—that is, spread the rumor that he was an FBI agent so that he'd be kicked out of the Party. If the FBI learned that a Party member was a homosexual, they would arrest him in order to embarrass the Party. More and more informers bent on disruption joined the Communist Party until it was like a dead log, hollowed out from within.

Hoover won. The American Communist Party lost. COINTELPRO was so successful, it became a joke. By 1960, it was common knowledge that half the Party members were FBI informants, spying on one another. To be fair, the Soviets were still eager to infiltrate their spies into America, so weakening the Party did make it more difficult for the Soviets to gather information and influence policy. If you judge by results, then, COINTELPRO worked. But Hoover was also leading the FBI deeper and deeper into the darkness. In the name of law, freedom, and democracy, his agents were using the strategies of the Soviet secret police. Officers of the United States government were working to hamper free thought, silence free speech, and prevent social protest. Hoover was becoming exactly what he detested: a force undermining the rule of law. And because of his clever filing system, no one was to ever know.

THE MYSTERY OF THE MOB

Hoover hated Robert F. Kennedy, the son of the immensely wealthy Joseph Kennedy and brother of the handsome rising star of the Democratic Party, John F. Kennedy. Hoover saw "Bobby" as an "arrogant whipper-snapper, who pushed around his family's money and power." That is not a bad description of Kennedy when Hoover first met him in the early 1950s. He was a rich kid who never had to spend a dime of his own money yet was a scrapper, a "runt," who battled everyone around him. You either admire a prep-school brawler like that or, like Hoover, you can't stand him.

Los Angeles crime boss Frank DeSimone (in dark suit) being taken to court for his arraignment after the Apalachin raid

In 1957, Kennedy was working for a Senate committee that was investigating crime in unions. Just then, a policeman in the small town of Apalachin, in upstate New York, stumbled on a national meeting of crime bosses. As the men scattered, the police gathered enough information to paint a picture for the public: Italian Americans from New York, Buffalo, Detroit, San Francisco, Los Angeles, Dallas, and Miami—many with long criminal records—were all in touch, carving up territories, making plans.

Kennedy stormed into the FBI, demanding information about the extremely suspicious men whose names were now all over the newspapers. The Bureau had nothing for him. Hoover still loved tales of his fight against the gangsters of the 1930s, but Dillinger, Nelson, Floyd, and the other gunmen of the time ran small local gangs. Hoover had little to say about organized crime. As he saw it, criminals cropped up here and there because individuals chose to be lawless and local officials looked the other way. Kennedy was saying just the opposite, that crime was a national problem, that there were syndicates, networks, of criminal bosses stretching across the nation. And why wasn't the FBI dealing with them?

Why, indeed? To those who believe in conspiracies, Hoover's resistance to going after what we now call the Mafia is a clue as bright as a blazing sun. One rumor has it that the mob had photos proving that he was a homosexual, a cross-dresser who liked to wear women's clothing, and used the pictures to blackmail him. Another claims that during his Stork Club days Hoover made a deal with a Mafia boss in which they agreed to stay out of each other's way. These popular myths are not true. The most likely reason is similar to why he did not want his men having to clash with white police chiefs in the South. Hoover let the local be local.

By law, the FBI was supposed to deal only with national crimes. So long as cities, neighborhoods, and small towns functioned relatively peacefully, Hoover did not feel a need to intervene. But that is not the only reason he had stayed away from mob bosses. On the one hand, Hoover would need tools. How was he going to get information about the Mafia? The organization was overwhelmingly Italian, and Hoover's agents were almost entirely white Protestants or Irish Catholics. He could use illegal wiretaps or bugs but not if he'd have to share power with other police forces. He would never let outsiders know about the Bureau's illegal activities. On the other hand, any agents who got in contact with the mob were in danger of being killed, bribed, or blackmailed. There was too much chance of failure and no clear path to success. Hoover would never take on a job like that unless a superior made him do it. In 1957, Robert Kennedy, the most annoying guy in the world, could point to the newspapers and demand action.

The meeting in upstate New York was evidence of precisely the hydra-headed monster Hoover had ignored. Going after the mob would be like challenging white policemen in the South: the FBI would have to be the arm of the nation challenging local power. The Bureau finally decided to get legal permission to use the skill it already had, planting electronic devices to record the mob leaders. Once again Hoover would be master of information. And the Mafia bosses had many interesting things to say—not only about their own plots and plans but also about a certain wealthy and handsome senator with political ambitions: Robert Kennedy's brother John.

17 THE DESCENT

At first glance, 1960 might seem to have been the worst year in Hoover's life. The America he had done so much to shape was slipping away. The Democrat John F. (Jack) Kennedy, the youngest elected president in American history, defeated Hoover's old ally Richard Nixon. College students in San Francisco began protesting against HUAC, a demonstration that Hoover termed a "Communist-inspired riot" but that was actually just the first hint of a decade of campus unrest. Frank Kameny, an openly gay man, made the case to the Supreme Court that firing a person for his or her sexual orientation was "no less illegal than discrimination based on religious or racial grounds." He lost but raised a legal issue that would become increasingly important.

Perhaps the biggest shift came in the arena where Hoover had done so much to shape public opinion: film. Hollywood decided to make a movie out of *Spartacus,* the Howard Fast novel Hoover had tried to suppress nine years

Frank Kameny organized the Mattachine Society of Washington to help gays and lesbians organize and speak out.

earlier. Worse yet, Dalton Trumbo, a writer who had been officially banned from the movies after he defied HUAC, was hired to write the script. The film was a full-color spectacular that went on to win four Academy Awards.

The incoming president aimed to bring a new spirit to Washington, and many were sure he would begin by replacing Hoover. The Harvard-educated Kennedy and his French-speaking wife were sophisticated, cultured, and eager for intellectual debate. It was as if, now that Hoover had reached retirement age, the grandchildren of John Reed had taken power and would usher him out the door. And by the end of 1960, word was out that Jack was going to appoint Bobby as attorney general, which is to say, as Hoover's boss. Wouldn't Bobby, who had clashed with Hoover over the mob three years earlier, want to bring in his own man as head of the FBI?

No. Hoover's meticulous files made sure of that. Throughout his adult life, Jack Kennedy had pursued women. Being married, a senator, and then a presidential candidate had done nothing to stop him. Not only had he been unfaithful, but he was also extremely reckless. One of his mistresses had been photographed with leading Nazis. Another, it would turn out, was a Communist spy. The FBI bug listening to mob bosses in Chicago turned up evidence that yet a third woman was involved with both Kennedy and a prominent Mafia don. The press heard rumors of many of these affairs but kept silent. Hoover gathered evidence of every single one of Jack's infidelities and made sure Bobby knew he had it. To protect his brother, Bobby would have to keep Hoover in office for as long as the director wanted the job.

One side of Hoover's lifelong quest succeeded: he had job protection even under a hostile administration. But his success was also his undoing. For it meant he would still be in office when enforcing the law would mean protecting the growing nonviolent movement for civil rights. His job would be to guard peaceful protesters such as Dr. Martin Luther King Jr. against people like himself.

Dr. King is the balance point in this book, in Hoover's life, and in our history. Throughout his career, Hoover had broken laws, violated rights, and misled those assigned to supervise him. But during much of that time, he had also protected the nation against potent and far more ruthless enemies. Though Hoover was deeply prejudiced and extremely devious, he was nothing like Stalin, who was a mass murderer. Both Hoover and Robert Kennedy came to believe that Dr. King was touched, tainted, perhaps controlled by those same deadly Communists. That is where Hoover went blind. He could not see in front of his own eyes; he could not understand the nation he was sworn to serve. He became lost in his own plots and schemes.

The blacklisting of Dalton Trumbo ended with his visible work on the Academy Award–winning film version of Spartacus. *Trumbo actually felt that Howard Fast was too pro-Communist, but he was a skilled writer who knew how to craft a compelling script.*

In 1962, the Kennedy brothers were slowly and carefully supporting King and the civil rights movement—not enough to please liberals, too much for conservatives. On January 8, the FBI informed Robert Kennedy that Stanley Levison, one of King's closest aides, was an important Communist. If that came out to the public, the Kennedys were doomed. They would lose, the civil rights bill they were planning to bring to Congress would lose, and King himself would lose. Several of Bobby Kennedy's assistants warned King that he must split from Levison. King listened, was polite, and politely refused.

The FBI's suspicion of Levison is a portrait of how Hoover's men saw the world. They had real evidence, but they were misled by deeply held beliefs and prejudices. They could no longer separate one from the other.

From the early 1950s on, two brothers intimately involved in bringing millions of dollars from the Soviets to the American Communist Party had been secretly feeding information to the Bureau. They reported that Levison, a wealthy businessman, was running the Party's most top-secret funds. But after 1955, Levison faded from the Party files, and in 1960 the Bureau even tried to recruit him to spy on his old Communist allies. Two years later, the

The Kennedy brothers map out their civil rights strategy. Just after this June 1963 talk, the president proposed a bill outlawing discrimination in public places. They were both terrified that Hoover was right—that Dr. King really did have a Communist as a close adviser—which would have doomed the bill, and probably the president's chances of being reelected.

FBI suddenly realized that Levison was back on the scene, working closely with Dr. King. Not only had he helped channel money to the civil rights movement, but he also played a key role in editing and even helping to write *Stride Toward Freedom,* the book Dr. King wrote about the Montgomery bus boycott. To the Bureau, this was both terribly alarming and crystal clear. The Party surely had sent Levison undercover—off their records but out into the world. King was a Communist pawn, being handled by their carefully white-washed agent.

Since the FBI was certain Levison was a Communist, it saw King's response in the worst possible light. King, one memo stated, "does not desire to be given the truth. The fact that he is a vicious liar is amply demonstrated in the fact he constantly associates with and takes instructions from Stanley Levison who is a hidden member of the Communist Party." The Bureau redoubled its efforts to find evidence that Levison was still a Communist, and Robert Kennedy approved. Agents snuck into Levison's New York office and planted a bug. It yielded nothing of interest, but the Bureau took that silence to mean that Levison was exceptionally devious. By May, both Levison and King were added to the FBI's new and updated list of people to be swept into detention in case of a national emergency. In June, a wiretap yielded sensational news: Levison suggested that King give an important job to Jack O'Dell, a young black man who had been a public member of the Communist Party. Didn't this show that the Party was maneuvering to position its men into key spots, building a cell just as its spies had done in the 1930s?

In the spring of 1963, Dr. King and his colleagues began planning for a massive March on Washington later that summer. Civil rights was becoming the central national issue, and on June 22, King came to the capital. In every private conference, people friendly to the movement kept saying the same thing: Levison is a Communist, a threat to everything you are trying to achieve. President Kennedy himself took Dr. King out for a private talk in the White House garden, away from all ears. He told King he must drop Levison. "I know Stanley," Dr. King replied, "and I can't believe this. You will have to prove it." The president agreed to produce the evidence.

The FBI could not help him: it had nothing new on Levison—just the opposite, in fact. On August 23, five days before the March on Washington, William Sullivan and his Domestic Intelligence Division delivered a lengthy report to Hoover that reviewed everything the Bureau knew about King, civil rights, and Communism. Sullivan's report was honest, clear, and devastating: the Communist Party was tiny and ineffectual, so while it had tried many times to reach and influence King, the entire effort was a complete failure. The FBI's own files cleared King and showed no recent links between Levison and the Party. Everything the Bureau had been feeding to friendly journalists, passing on to the attorney general, and telling the president, was wrong.

Hoover blew up.

The director could not believe his eyes. "I for one," he snapped, "can't ignore the memos re King." The excellent historian Richard Powers, who has studied Hoover deeply, thinks the director was sincerely puzzled because what Sullivan was telling him was the direct opposite of everything his agents had been saying. "I have," Hoover wrote to Tolson, "certainly been misled by previous memos which clearly showed communist penetration of the racial movement. . . . We are wasting manpower and money investigating CP effort in racial matter if the attached is correct." Perhaps Hoover really would have been willing to totally change the Bureau's view of King if his men had stuck to their word. But when Hoover rejected the report, Sullivan and his entire department panicked.

Sullivan knew what happened to agents, even the most favored ones, when, like Melvin Purvis, they crossed the director. Their careers were over, their lives ruined. "The Director is correct," Sullivan quickly wrote back. King is "the most dangerous Negro of the future in this Nation from the standpoint of communism, the Negro and national security." Sullivan needed to write a new report, many new reports, as fast as possible; he needed to prove to Hoover that he knew King to be a liar, a fraud, and a Communist pawn. Indeed, he now claimed that the Bureau needed to set new rules for itself in order to deal with such a vile enemy: "It may be unrealistic to limit ourselves as we have been doing to legalistic proofs."

If Dr. Powers is right, Hoover was personally willing to be wrong, but he had created a Bureau that was so rigid, fearful, and habitually dishonest that his agents would much rather feed him pleasing lies than tell him upsetting truths. He himself was open to new insights, but the organization he had created was not. Hoover had turned the FBI into a lie machine.

Would Hoover really have been willing to drop the King-Communism connection if Sullivan had stuck by his original report? That seems unlikely. Back in the 1930s, he chose to hide reports that showed the America First Committee was totally independent of the Nazis. He passed along only information that fit what he assumed FDR wanted to see. This situation was similar. He would approve only reports that agreed that King was under Communist influence. Knowing that, Sullivan and others flooded Hoover with memos stating that the Communists were controlling King. Finally, in October, the director softened. "I am glad," he penciled on one, "you recognize at last that there exists such influence." The more Sullivan insisted that King was "a fraud, demagogue, and moral scoundrel," the better Hoover seemed to feel. "I am glad," he wrote back to Sullivan, "that the 'light' has finally, though dismally delayed, come to the Domestic Intelligence Division. I struggled for months to get over the fact that the communists were taking over the racial movement, but our experts here couldn't or wouldn't see it."

That nod of approval suggests that Hoover's mind had been made up for a long, long time. The Sullivan report shocked him—if only because it showed his men being willing to defy what they knew he wanted. It took him some time to calm down and forgive his own agents. But he would never have accepted anything other than confirmation of his own firm beliefs. If this view is correct, Hoover was lost in his own nightmares and no one could have shaken him awake.

Lie machine or haunted house: either way, Hoover and his FBI could not recognize—did not even consider—the other way to look at the link between a former Communist such as Levison and King. It is not that devious Communists were using the civil rights movement. Rather, idealists who believed in racial integration at first turned to Communism, then later saw a better path through Dr. King and the civil rights movement. The connection between Party and protest was the vision of a better America King voiced at the March on Washington, not a plot for Communist revolution hatched in secret.

Look back to the two versions of American history in the first chapter. Hoover was so devoted to the pageant of American glory—the proud story of the individual pioneer and businessman—that he could only see the alternative as coming from an alien enemy. He was wrong. You can be a severe critic of America and still be a loyal American. Hoover was blind to that idea, and no one in the FBI was willing to risk challenging him. In his mad effort to protect his country, Hoover increasingly violated the most basic American rights, starting with Dr. King.

The FBI could not give the president the proof that King demanded. But it had plenty of evidence that King was continuing to lean on Levison for advice. If Hoover was right, if King was defying the Kennedys to protect a Communist, that meant disaster for the administration. Robert Kennedy was concerned in August, more worried in September, and in October, he decided to act. On October 10, he authorized the FBI to use electronic surveillance on Dr. Martin Luther King. He was desperate to know if any "information developed regarding King's communist connections." By November, agents were listening in on Dr. King twenty-four hours a day, seven days a week. The American government was spying on the leader of the civil rights movement. Those taps yielded secrets—but not the ones the Bureau expected.

"DESTROY THE BURRHEAD"

By December, Sullivan was back in Hoover's good graces and seeking out ever-new ways to discredit King. He called a conference of key FBI agents to figure out the best way of "neutralizing King as an effective Negro leader." They were out to "expose King for the clerical fraud and Marxist he is at the first opportunity."

In January, the FBI began planting bugs in the various hotels King visited as he traveled around the country. The tapes recorded King making raunchy jokes and having affairs with various women. King was not only a moral leader; he was also an ordained minister. Yet here was clear evidence of immorality and infidelity. According to Sullivan, Hoover felt sure that this evidence would "destroy the burrhead." We cannot know precisely what the tapes contain, since they are sealed until 2027, but every expert is certain they are authentic.

The tapes changed the FBI's focus. They produced no evidence of Communist influence. But Sullivan, in particular, was outraged. The King

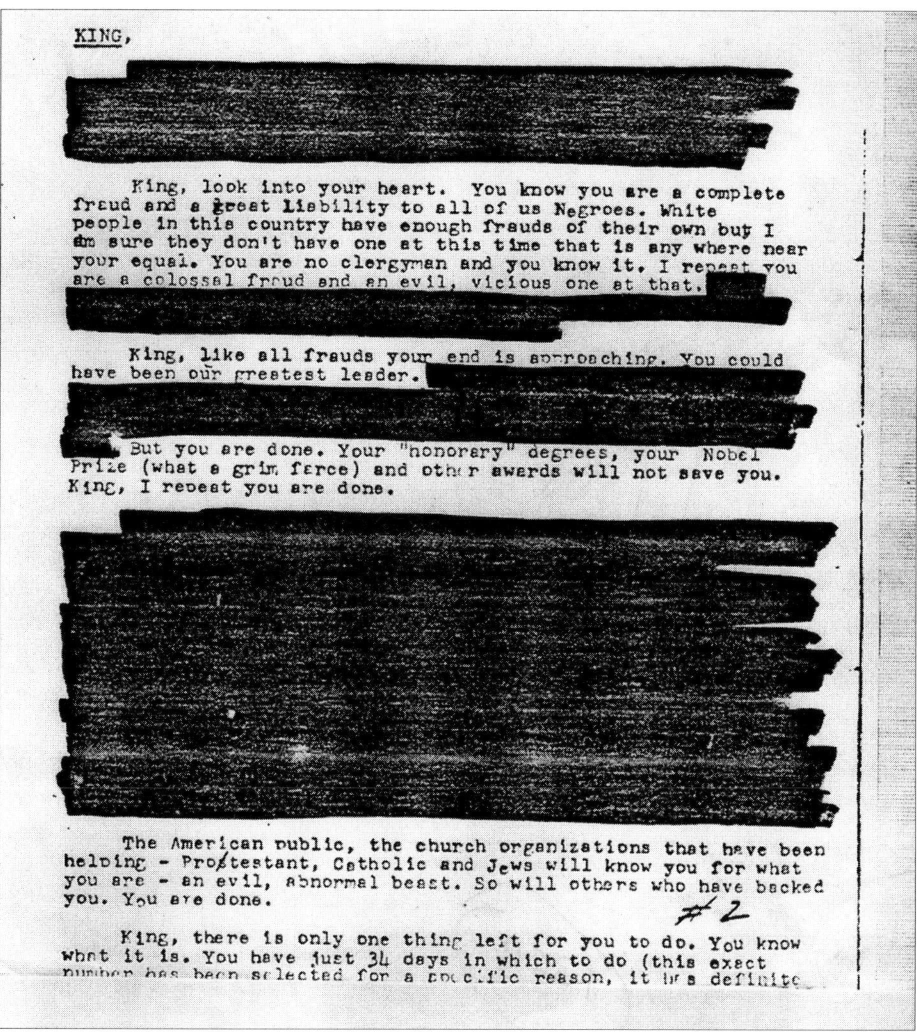
KING,

King, look into your heart. You know you are a complete fraud and a great liability to all of us Negroes. White people in this country have enough frauds of their own but I am sure they don't have one at this time that is any where near your equal. You are no clergyman and you know it. I repeat you are a colossal fraud and an evil, vicious one at that.

King, like all frauds your end is approaching. You could have been our greatest leader.

But you are done. Your "honorary" degrees, your Nobel Prize (what a grim farce) and other awards will not save you. King, I repeat you are done.

The American public, the church organizations that have been helping - Protestant, Catholic and Jews will know you for what you are - an evil, abnormal beast. So will others who have backed you. You are done.

#2

King, there is only one thing left for you to do. You know what it is. You have just 34 days in which to do (this exact number has been selected for a specific reason, it has definite

Here is a second FBI redaction of the letter sent to Dr. King—compare it with the version on the second page of the prologue.

who was heard in the hotel rooms was the opposite of the man the public admired. The FBI now tried to spread word about King's character. They gave transcripts to Robert Kennedy and to Lyndon Johnson, who had become president when JFK was assassinated. Kennedy was disturbed, but perhaps because of his own experience with his brother, he did not judge King by his private life. Johnson, who had had affairs of his own, treated the tapes as amusing. The FBI was not able to get key people to turn against King based on the tapes. So they tried one more tack.

In August 1964, scholars believe that Sullivan, pretending to be a black

American, wrote the letter that is summarized in the prologue of this book. The FBI made a master tape with selections from its recordings of King, packaged it with Sullivan's letter, and had it sent to King and to his wife. "King," it read, "look into your heart. You know you are a complete fraud and a great liability to all of us Negroes. . . . You are no clergyman and you know it. I repeat you are a colossal fraud and an evil, vicious one at that. . . . There is only one thing left for you to do. You know what it is. . . . You are done. There is but one way out for you. You better take it before your filthy, abnormal, fraudulent self is bared to the nation."

King guessed that FBI agents had made the recordings, and he understood their aim: "they are out to break me." Mrs. King was equally devoted to the civil rights struggle and knew that to show any public reaction would only please its enemies. But, according to King's Pulitzer Prize–winning biographer, David Garrow, King was also haunted by his own moral failings. "Every now and then," King said in one sermon, "you'll be unfaithful to those that you should be faithful to." Dr. King never claimed to be perfect. In fact, he always felt there were "two Martin Luther Kings" and they were at odds. "It's a mixture in human nature," he said. "Because we are two selves, there is a civil war going on within each of us." The real Dr. King was not a plaster saint, not an image giving a speech about a dream. He was a flawed man who was not faithful to his wife. He was as divided, as pulled in two, as in conflict with himself, as anyone else. To King, the tapes were a record of his weakness, of the clash between his ideals and his desires.

King did have secrets. His private life was at odds with his position of moral leadership. That could have given Hoover power, as other secrets so often had. Yet both Dr. and Mrs. King understood that inspiring leaders can have imperfect private lives. They realized that sometimes an ideal is more important than a secret. The change in America was not going to be derailed by one man's personal weakness. In their desperate blackmail letter, which King was sure was meant to push him toward suicide, Sullivan, Hoover, and the FBI could not see that. They detested King and resisted change. They were out of step with their own time, and they went further into their own private world of calculation and plot.

18 COINTELPRO

The assassination of President Kennedy in 1963 was a first indication of the increasingly violent mood of the decade. In the South, the civil rights struggle brought out both Klan members with guns and policemen with dogs, batons, and fire hoses. Overseas, the United States was increasingly involved in a brutal war in Vietnam, which inspired intense clashes on American college campuses. But the worst violence came in the poor black neighborhoods of large cities. Between 1965 and 1967, Los Angeles, Chicago, Cleveland, Newark, Brooklyn, Omaha, Baltimore, San Francisco, and Detroit erupted in flames. The FBI turned to ever-more-secret means to try to maintain control and calm the nation.

Sullivan led the next round of COINTELPRO activities in what might seem an unexpected direction: against the Ku Klux Klan. Starting in late 1964, the FBI paid informants to join the Klan, as they had the Communist Party. Then, as Klan members grew suspicious, they used the snitch jacket, spreading rumors that Klan leaders were FBI agents. The FBI was working to track, hamper, and ultimately hobble the Klan. But by doing that from within, it took another step into dispensing its own justice.

Hoover defined the new mission of COINTELPRO operations: to "'neutralize' the effectiveness of civil rights, New Left, antiwar and black liberation groups." "New Left" was a term of the time that referred to college students who were not members of the Communist Party but were devoted to the rights and needs of workers and the poor. "Neutralize," the same word Sullivan had used for King, was now applied to causes that were inspiring a rising generation of Americans. Hoover later added another movement to his list of evildoers: all feminists, members of the women's movement, he said, "should be viewed as part of the enemy, a challenge to American values." The FBI set out to undermine and fragment every voice of opposition in America so that the nation could return to the place Hoover had eyed with such contentment from the shuffleboard court of the Del Charro in 1953. He was like a mad doctor who is so determined to battle a disease that he sets about to kill his patients.

In 1967, the FBI began seeking informants in any black organization it could reach, no matter how small. Everyone from taxi drivers to bookstore owners was asked to report on attitudes in black communities. The following year, COINTELPRO was expanded to expressly seek out black nationalist groups. Both Dr. King and Bobby Kennedy were assassinated that year, and some people gave up hope of integrating America. Instead, they listened to

This image of Huey Newton, one of the founders of the Black Panther Party, was a popular poster in the 1960s. "The racist dog policemen," Newton wrote, "must withdraw immediately from our communities, cease their wanton murder, brutality and torture of Black People, or face the wrath of the armed people." The FBI was fostering conflict in black communities, but Newton had his own violent streak and was murdered by a drug dealer.

leaders who argued that blacks needed to arm themselves, take control of their own neighborhoods, and separate from whites.

The black nationalists rejected nonviolence. To them, King had been weak. In every word and deed, they were out to show they were tough and could handle themselves. They meant to inspire fear, and they did. COINTELPRO used this against them. Informants were paid to join groups and encourage them to battle other militants, to get more violent, to turn on one another. According to a later government report, the Bureau wanted to create "shootings, beatings, and a high degree of unrest."

As rumors about FBI infiltration of black nationalist movements began to spread, paid allies once again used the snitch jacket—accusing others of working for the FBI. The FBI, the organization charged with protecting Americans, was doing its best to set off conflicts, to turn people against one another, to make sure that black organizations could not work together. And then it extended the same tactics to largely white college campuses.

In 1968, COINTELPRO was expanded yet again, this time to go after students protesting against the Vietnam War and seeking to change American society. Agents set out to embarrass and harass student and faculty leaders and to turn administrators against them. The FBI sent letters to the parents of college students who were protesting against the war—as if the Bureau were a principal's office sending a note about a disruptive child. In order to set the two against each other, the Bureau also tried to convince black nationalist groups that white student groups were racist. Any lie would do, so long as it served to divide students and diminish their antiwar activism.

Hoover now sent informants to infiltrate and report on the women's liberation movement. Unfortunately, their reports reflected their own concerns: "One of the interesting aspects about other delegates' dress was the extreme fuzzy appearance of their hair. Some said this . . . was gotten by braiding and leaving it that way while it was wet until it dried. Then they would take out the braid. From the looks of their hair, they apparently really didn't bother to try and comb it out afterward." As shocking as fuzzy hair may have been to this FBI source, it was hardly a matter of national security.

With reports like this—on braiding, not bombing—the FBI faced the

PHOTO DOSSIER:
In the late 1960s and early 1970s, between images of the war in Vietnam and deadly clashes in cities and on college campuses, revolution was in the air. Burned-out cities began to look like war zones, and American soldiers fired on fellow citizens.

Right: Black Panther leader Fred Hampton, killed under suspicious circumstances

Below: One of the worst city conflicts in American history started in Detroit on June 23, 1967, with a mishandled police raid. In five days, forty-three people were killed and more than 1,100 were injured.

A captured Viet Cong prisoner awaits interrogation by U.S. forces in 1967.

This Pulitzer Prize–winning photo captures the horror on the face of Mary Ann Vecchio when the Ohio National Guard shot and killed four students and wounded nine others during a 1970 Kent State University protest against the war in Vietnam.

same dilemma that had arisen when it studied the America First Committee and later Dr. King. Its own best evidence showed the movement was "mainly concerned with male chauvinism and didn't seem to require any investigation," but Hoover would not listen. He insisted that "interwoven with its goals for equal rights for women is the advocation of violence to achieve these goals."

There was indeed an air of revolution and violence in all the groups Hoover sought to undermine: the New Left, the black nationalists, even the most radical feminists. When William Wordsworth wrote about the "bliss" of being young in the midst of a revolution, he was describing a kind of intoxication, being drunk with hope, fear, and rage. In the late 1960s and early '70s, to be extreme became fashionable and toying with violence was popular. In that mood it was very easy to hate—the government, capitalists, parents, white people, men, straight people. It was as if America were having a national temper tantrum during which destroying everything was much more exciting than stopping and cleaning up the wreckage.

In that sense, Hoover was right. The FBI did have real enemies to contend with. There were in fact people and groups collecting arms, building bombs, and advocating revolution. Violence—from the murder of the nation's most famous leaders, to burning buildings in major cities—was in the air. America was in danger of fracturing: black against white, students against adults, prowar against antiwar. In New York City, radical black nationalists were indeed plotting to ignite race war by murdering moderate leaders and then spreading the rumor that the government was responsible. Soviet agents, using tactics similar to those of COINTELPRO, circulated rumors of Hoover's homosexuality and used fake stationery to link the FBI to extreme right-wing organizations. Some of the fog of confusion over Hoover's secrets results from deliberate Soviet efforts to undermine him.

Feminism, war, and revolution all blended in the language and slogans of a violent era. The quotation in this poster comes from a delegation of Vietnamese women at a conference in Canada.

INTERSTATE FLIGHT - MOB ACTION; RIOT; CONSPIRACY

WANTED BY FBI

The persons shown here are active members of the militant Weatherman faction of the Students for a Democratic Society - SDS.

Federal warrants have been issued at Chicago, Illinois, concerning these individuals, charging them with a variety of Federal violations including interstate flight to avoid prosecution, mob action, Antiriot Laws and conspiracy. Some of these individuals were also charged in an indictment returned 7/23/70, at Detriot, Michigan, with conspiracy to violate Federal Bombing and Gun Control Laws.

These individuals should be considered dangerous because of their known advocacy and use of explosives, reported acquisition of firearms and incendiary devices, and known propensity for violence.

If you have information concerning these persons please contact your local FBI Office.

William Charles Ayers
W/M, 25, 5-10, 170
brn hair, brn eyes

Kathie Boudin
W/F, 28, 5-4, 128
brn hair, blue eyes

Judith Alice Clark
W/F, 20, 5-3, 125
brn hair, brn eyes

Bernardine Rae Dohrn
W/F, 28, 5-5, 125
drk brn hair, brn eyes

The Weathermen were a faction of student radicals who turned ever more violent and extreme in their beliefs and actions.

America faced real threats. But all the FBI could do was to turn to ever-more-devious and illegal efforts to undermine groups it feared, disliked, or opposed. The Bureau's plots relied on illegal tactics that only worsened the divisions in society. The Bureau had become the problem it was designed to investigate and expose. Ironically, the FBI itself was now so filled with secrets that it became a prime target for the very tactics it had used.

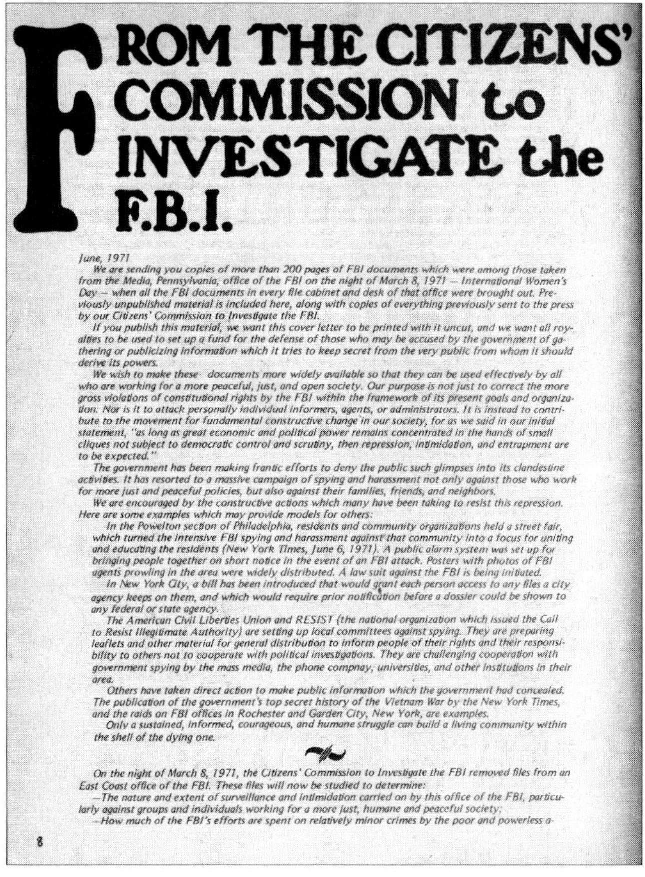

FROM THE CITIZENS' COMMISSION to INVESTIGATE the F.B.I.

June, 1971

We are sending you copies of more than 200 pages of FBI documents which were among those taken from the Media, Pennsylvania, office of the FBI on the night of March 8, 1971 — International Women's Day — when all the FBI documents in every file cabinet and desk of that office were brought out. Previously unpublished material is included here, along with copies of everything previously sent to the press by our Citizens' Commission to Investigate the FBI.

If you publish this material, we want this cover letter to be printed with it uncut, and we want all royalties to be used to set up a fund for the defense of those who may be accused by the government of gathering or publicizing information which it tries to keep secret from the very public from whom it should derive its powers.

We wish to make these documents more widely available so that they can be used effectively by all who are working for a more peaceful, just, and open society. Our purpose is not just to correct the more gross violations of constitutional rights by the FBI within the framework of its present goals and organization. Nor is it to attack personally individual informers, agents, or administrators. It is instead to contribute to the movement for fundamental constructive change in our society, for as we said in our initial statement, "as long as great economic and political power remains concentrated in the hands of small cliques not subject to democratic control and scrutiny, then repression, intimidation, and entrapment are to be expected."

The government has been making frantic efforts to deny the public such glimpses into its clandestine activities. It has resorted to a massive campaign of spying and harassment not only against those who work for more just and peaceful policies, but also against their families, friends, and neighbors.

We are encouraged by the constructive actions which many have been taking to resist this repression. Here are some examples which may provide models for others:

In the Powelton section of Philadelphia, residents and community organizations held a street fair, which turned the intensive FBI spying and harassment against that community into a focus for uniting and educating the residents (New York Times, June 6, 1971). A public alarm system was set up for bringing people together on short notice in the event of an FBI attack. Posters with photos of FBI agents prowling in the area were widely distributed. A law suit against the FBI is being initiated.

In New York City, a bill has been introduced that would grant each person access to any files a city agency keeps on them, and which would require prior notification before a dossier could be shown to any federal or state agency.

The American Civil Liberties Union and RESIST (the national organization which issued the Call to Resist Illegitimate Authority) are setting up local committees against spying. They are preparing leaflets and other material for general distribution to inform people of their rights and their responsibility to others not to cooperate with political investigations. They are challenging cooperation with government spying by the mass media, the phone compnay, universities, and other institutions in their area.

Others have taken direct action to make public information which the government had concealed. The publication of the government's top secret history of the Vietnam War by the New York Times, and the raids on FBI offices in Rochester and Garden City, New York, are examples.

Only a sustained, informed, courageous, and humane struggle can build a living community within the shell of the dying one.

On the night of March 8, 1971, the Citizens' Commission to Investigate the FBI removed files from an East Coast office of the FBI. These files will now be studied to determine:

—The nature and extent of surveillance and intimidation carried on by this office of the FBI, particularly against groups and individuals working for a more just, humane and peaceful society;

—How much of the FBI's efforts are spent on relatively minor crimes by the poor and powerless a-

8

By breaking into an FBI office in Media, Pennsylvania, critics of the Bureau captured documents that led to the exposure of COINTELPRO. This flyer accompanied the files as they were sent to news agencies.

On March 6, 1971, the Citizens Commission to Investigate the FBI did a black-bag job on an FBI office in Media, Pennsylvania. That is, they broke in, grabbed pages of documents, and soon published them. The files revealed wiretaps and other surveillance. One suggested that the FBI should come onto campuses and interview students in order create fear and to "get the point across there is an FBI agent behind every mailbox." The file contained one word no one outside of the Bureau had ever seen before, COINTELPRO. Newsman Carl Stern of NBC-TV was curious what the term meant and began the legal process to force the FBI to explain.

Opposite: Hoover sitting comfortably with President Nixon in December 1971. By this time, Hoover had ensured that he would have his FBI job for life but refused to involve the agency in the crimes that would lead to the president's resignation.

There is something almost too perfect about this sequence of events, which seems to fit better in a fantasy novel than in reality. Hoover had used newspapers, comic strips, books, radio, movies, and TV to sell his story of the FBI. But now, in the little town called Media, a one-word clue leaked out, which caught the interest of an alert TV reporter. That first clue would eventually help unravel the whole world of FBI illegality. Instead of repeating Hoover's story of the heroic FBI defending America from alien enemies, the media was about to begin revealing how the FBI had been the alien undermining the principles of American democracy.

Hoover was spared having to see that disaster unfold. On May 2, 1972, J. Edgar Hoover died in his sleep — safe in the knowledge that he was still the head of the FBI.

HOOVER'S HERITAGE: WATERGATE

Hoover's story ends with his death, yet there is a coda, a twist that had been set in motion four years earlier. Richard Nixon was elected president in 1968 and reelected four years later, which was seemingly the best news for his old friend and ally J. Edgar Hoover. Hoover was well past retirement age,

In 1967, Hollywood returned to the story of Bonnie and Clyde *(see pages 34–35)**, only this time the audience was encouraged to admire the attractive, youthful rebels. Here, peace activists have pasted the faces of President Johnson and his wife over those of film stars Warren Beatty and Faye Dunaway, to portray LBJ as a cold-blooded killer for his role in the Vietnam War.*

but he knew his job was safe. His new boss gave him a steady stream of illegal assignments, such as wiretapping newspaper reporters who dared to criticize the president, or tracking down who among them were homosexuals. As usual, this secret work padded Hoover's own files to use against Nixon, if the need arose. But there was a hint of trouble.

Hoover's caution flags were flying: he saw that courts were leaning toward protecting privacy and against the government. So from 1965 to '66, he told his agents to stop their black-bag jobs and illegal wiretaps unless they were given explicit orders by the president or the attorney general. He was an old hedgehog burrowing deeper into his cave. But by 1969, Nixon was furious at the growing antiwar protest movement and demanded proof that the college students were the tools of international Communism. He wanted all the arms of government, including the FBI, the Central Intelligence Agency (CIA), and the Defense Intelligence Agency (DIA), to work together to find that evidence, by any means necessary. Tom Huston, an eager aide to Nixon, worked with William Sullivan to draft a plan under which Hoover's rules limiting the FBI's illegal activities would be repealed.

Hoover read the shifting mood of the nation. He saw the danger in using his old tricks. Nixon was in office. But if he lost, if power shifted in Congress, there would be investigations. The risk was too high. He also resisted the idea of working with any other agencies. The director, the master of break-ins, spying, and blackmail, carefully pointed out every action in the plan that would be illegal. Hoover put all the risk in Nixon's lap, just as he had waited for FDR's secret nod to go after "subversives."

Hoover had the president in a corner, and Nixon knew it. He could not fire the man who had already broken the law for him. And he could not push him to violate more laws unless he made himself directly responsible. Nixon dropped the whole idea.

On June 17, six weeks after Hoover's death, a shadowy group of men tried to break in and plant bugging devices in the Democratic National Committee offices in the Watergate complex in Washington. A night watchman saw the bumbling men, and the story exploded in the press. Presidents back to at least Herbert Hoover had requested illegal political invasions like this, but what could be swept under the rug in 1930 made headlines in 1972. When the FBI began to investigate, the Justice Department kept dragging its heels, blocking the Bureau from following its own leads. As two reporters from the *Washington Post* set out to learn what had really happened, they began to get tips from an extremely cautious but clearly well-informed source they code named Deep Throat.

Someone who knew how to disguise himself and keep a step ahead of anyone on his tail was giving clues to the reporters so that they could figure out who was behind the break-in. The trail Deep Throat mapped out led to the very top, to President Nixon himself, who was forced to resign. (The action-packed story of how reporters Carl Bernstein and Bob Woodward followed Deep Throat's clues is played out in the 1976 Oscar-winning film *All the President's Men.*)

Hoover had nothing to do with the break-in. In fact, some believe Nixon turned to amateurs because Hoover was so reluctant to be part of the Huston plan. But in a sense, Watergate, as the scandal came to be called, destroyed everything Hoover had spent a lifetime building and hiding. We now know that Deep Throat was Mark Felt, the lifetime agent who had rehearsed his handshake with Hoover so carefully back in 1954. Felt believed in the Bureau and was upset that it was being prevented from doing its job by the White House. He also personally felt snubbed that he was not named to head the

WANTED

APPREHENDED
JAMES McCORD
APPREHENDED
DWIGHT CHAPIN
APPREHENDED
H.R. HALDEMAN
APPREHENDED
JOHN MITCHELL
APPREHENDED
JOHN ERLICHMAN
APPREHENDED
MAURICE STANS
APPREHENDED
EUGENIO MARTINEZ
APPREHENDED
G. GORDON LIDDY
APPREHENDED
CHARLES COLSON
APPREHENDED
HERBERT KALMBACH
APPREHENDED
JOHN DEAN
APPREHENDED
ROBERT MARDIAN
APPREHENDED
JEB MAGRUDER
RICHARD M. NIXON
APPREHENDED
BERNARD L. BARKER
APPREHENDED
VIRGILIO GONZALEZ
APPREHENDED
DONALD SEGRETTI
APPREHENDED
FRANK A. STURGIS
APPREHENDED
E. HOWARD HUNT JR.
APPREHENDED
HUGH SLOAN JR.

FBI after Hoover died. Hoover had built an agency that was entirely focused on him—how he wanted hair parted, shoes tied, memos written, cases investigated, and results reported. William Sullivan and Mark Felt both hoped to become the new director; neither was given the job. But no one would ever be The Director again. Once Hoover was gone, the Lie Machine was at war with itself, and the secrets began to come out.

In the aftermath of Watergate, the media and Congress demanded to find hidden FBI files and make them available to the public. A crime Hoover refused to commit opened the door to revealing the nearly fifty years of criminal activity that was his legacy.

The American public learned about COINTELPRO in 1973 and '74; the House and Senate investigated the Bureau in 1975 and '76. "The United States," the final Senate committee report concluded, "must not adopt the tactics of the enemy. Means are as important as ends." By the end of the 1970s, Hoover's reputation had changed completely. The public was far more interested in whether he was a cross-dresser and/or a homosexual than in honoring him as a guardian against Communism. In recent years, popular culture—so often Hoover's ally—has turned against him. Documentaries—some serious, some retelling rumors—have dug into his secrets. The film *Public Enemies* finally made Melvin Purvis a hero, while the Clint Eastwood biopic *J. Edgar* centers on the supposed love between Hoover and Clyde Tolson.

Hoover's life goal was to live up to his mother's standards while avoiding his father's fate: to uphold law, oppose disorder, show no weakness, and never be in danger of losing his job. He succeeded. But in doing so, he failed. The bureau he built around himself as a perfect defense cracked and crumbled after he died. And yet, because he worked so hard, lived so long, and left such a mark on American history, his life matters. He showed us the price of feeling safe.

Opposite: This image mimics the FBI's wanted posters but depicts those involved in Watergate-related illegal activities. Only the president has not been "apprehended." Hoover had been canny enough to keep the FBI out of this scandal, but it was too late to guard all the secrets in his carefully managed files.

EPILOGUE

Master of Deceit, Then and Now

In 1958, a book publisher owned by Hoover's Del Charro host Clint Murchison released *Masters of Deceit,* a book warning of the dangers of Communism and purportedly written by Hoover. In fact it had been crafted by a team of writers at the FBI, and yet when the book sold millions of copies, the earnings went to Hoover and a few close associates. That book gives this one its title.

As we have seen, Hoover was masterful at hiding his illegal activities while convincing Americans that he was the guardian of the law. But he also mastered the deceits of others. Through crime waves, war, and Cold War, he did protect the country by helping to expose its hidden enemies. He was both a deceiver himself and a relentless investigator of the deceptions of others. But this book is not and should not be just about Hoover.

Hoover drew his strength from the lies others needed to tell. His story, then, is a portrait of the beliefs and attitudes of the times in which he lived. If, like Dr. King, you weren't scared, Hoover's taps were useless. The more silent the press was about an important person's private life, the more rumors, gossip, and secrets there were for Hoover to collect. In a sense, then, this whole story is not about lies people tried to hide but rather what the media was willing to expose. We as a nation were the Masters of Deceit.

Today, gossip and exposure have won. The Internet is crammed with sites detailing the affairs and imperfections of every possible public figure. That is normal: we are curious about one another, and especially about what goes on in private, behind closed doors. And yet the din of rumor and gossip can also take over, drowning out serious discussions and debates. The media is no longer controlled by people who could decide what to hide and what to reveal; it is controlled by us, all the time. And that leads back to Hoover.

Hoover provided the security Americans wanted. Our beliefs about what was acceptable or not acceptable—what could be shown in public and what had to be guarded in private—shaped the secrets he could gather. Hoover talked about the "specter" of racial intermarriage, and in his day many families—including perhaps his own—did keep their ancestry secret. Only in recent years have we looked back at our long heritage of racial mixing and realized that blending is something to celebrate rather than hide. The alert reader may have noticed another "specter" that haunted the Age of Lies: homosexuality.

The America in which Hoover rose to power treated homosexuality as a secret muttered in private. Yet, as the Kinsey Report showed, it was a common part of human experience. The pressure between what was half known and what could be said led to many, many rumors. For example, those on the left insisted that McCarthy picked up men (which was probably not true), while those on the right spread questionable rumors about the Democrat Adlai Stevenson, who twice ran against Dwight Eisenhower for president. Of course people endlessly gossiped about Hoover and Tolson.

Starting in the 1960s, homosexuality itself began to come out of the closet. Individuals stated openly whom they loved, a more general recognition of the fact that many American men and women wanted to live with, love, and build families with people of their own sex. That was no longer a rumor, a suspicion, a source of shame; it was announced as a fact of human life. Key court rulings in 1965 and 1969 said government agencies could not fire employees just because of their sexual orientation, challenging the entire "security risk" argument. As homosexuality became more accepted, one more secret lost some of its power; it was no longer quite the same source of fear and blackmail.

Most probably, Hoover could not accept his own feelings toward men; he could not even admit those yearnings to himself. He lived in a world of good and evil, purity and degeneracy. Stanley Levison could only be a Communist, not an idealist. Dr. King could only be a fraud, not a flawed leader. Communism itself could only be an incitement to lawlessness, violence, and corruption, not a useful critique of inequalities in society. For many Americans in Hoover's day, that kind of firm line was reassuring. We as a nation wanted our heroes and villains, our manly men and feminine women, our bright public face and invisible private lives. Hoover gave us the security we wanted.

What secrets do we have today? What kind of security do we want now?

In your lifetime, we will again face terrible threats and even perhaps experience unthinkable crimes. What will make us safe? How can we preserve Louis Post's careful attention to fair play, Senator Smith's sense of conscience, the ability to see a full human being, which Dr. King preached, when we feel rage and terror? Hoover's story teaches us two lessons: Fear allows secrecy in the name of defense. And that which is hidden grows malignant. When the people we rely on to defend us are permitted to hide their actions, it is all too easy for them to cover up their own crimes and breed a culture of fear. Personal emotions—fear of homosexual desire, prejudice against African Americans—are given the name of national security. Strength does not require silence.

But we must also remember that some threats are real. The Venona decryption showed a larger web of Soviet spying than liberals wanted to admit. The Communists murdered millions in the Soviet Union, and even more in China. In America, the Communist Party demanded obedience from its members, telling them how to write, act, and even think. Radicals in the 1960s did preach violent revolution, and some waved the flag of liberation only to take advantage of their followers. And of course Al Qaeda did attack us on September 11, 2001. Silence in the face of real threats is cowardice.

TORTURE

Mitchell Palmer and the young J. Edgar Hoover rounded up immigrants in order to deport them. Immediately after the September 11 attacks, some 762 individuals with apparently Arabic names were arrested without charges made against them. Some were placed in twenty-three-hour-a-day solitary confinement. Every one of them was eventually released, since they had no ties to terrorism. The Patriot Act extended the roundup. It allowed the government to sweep up and question immigrants, and especially those from Muslim nations. Many immigrants who had come here to find work and had outdated or inadequate documents were suddenly in danger of being kicked out of the country. This was so even if they had been here nearly their whole lives, spoke only English, had married here and had children or grandchildren here. Colleges were pressured to give the government personal information about their foreign students even if there was no specific reason to be concerned about those individuals. Librarians were asked to report on who took out which books (they refused). To Hoover and Palmer, being Russian and Jewish was cause for suspicion; after 2001, to be a Muslim immigrant in America was equally suspect. Ten years later, Congress held hearings on radical Islam in America that reminded critics of the HUAC sessions on Communism.

In 2001, our government believed that protecting America was so important that we could do nearly anything in order to catch a suspected terrorist. In fact, the government went further than Hoover ever dared. For he never used torture.

America was the first nation in the world to oppose torture and has signed many international treaties spelling out the rights of our enemies. In 2001, our government swept those rights away. In the face of the new threat,

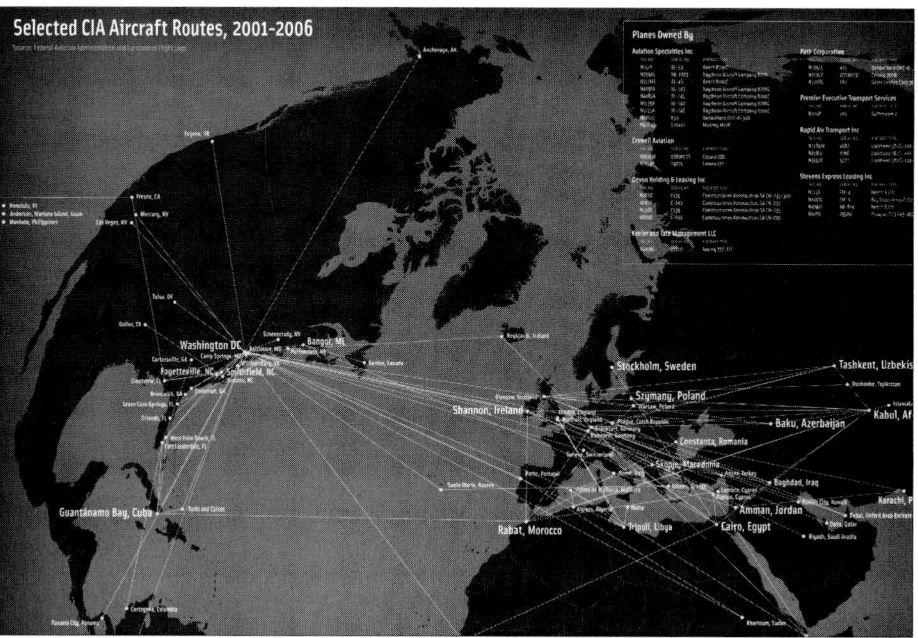

This map shows the destinations to which the U.S. government secretly flew terrorist suspects. In these places, they could be questioned and tortured without having any recourse to legal protection.

our leaders believed, there were no limits. If we needed to get someone to spill his secrets, we could nearly drown him until, gasping for breath, fighting for life, he would speak. That practice is called waterboarding. As the prize-winning reporter Jane Mayer explained, "The President could argue that torture was legal because he had authorized it." The president was no longer checked and balanced by Congress, the courts, or by treaties his predecessors had signed. He was above the law. That is precisely the authorization that Hoover claimed he received from FDR and that opened the door to so many FBI crimes and cover-ups.

As a candidate, Barack Obama officially rejected this entire view of how to keep America strong and safe. And yet ever since he took office, members of his own administration have been deeply divided over exactly what we can and cannot do. We are fighting enemies who are not a nation but a loose network. They don't wear uniforms. Whom do we define as a terrorist? Sites on the Internet tell unhappy young people that they need to join the global holy war against America. Unfortunately some have responded to this new "answer" and tried to spread violence and death. How much freedom of speech should these Internet terrormongers have? Should we monitor who goes to their websites? If so, aren't we doing exactly what Hoover did in filling out his file cards showing nodes of potential Communist subversion? What is the price of security?

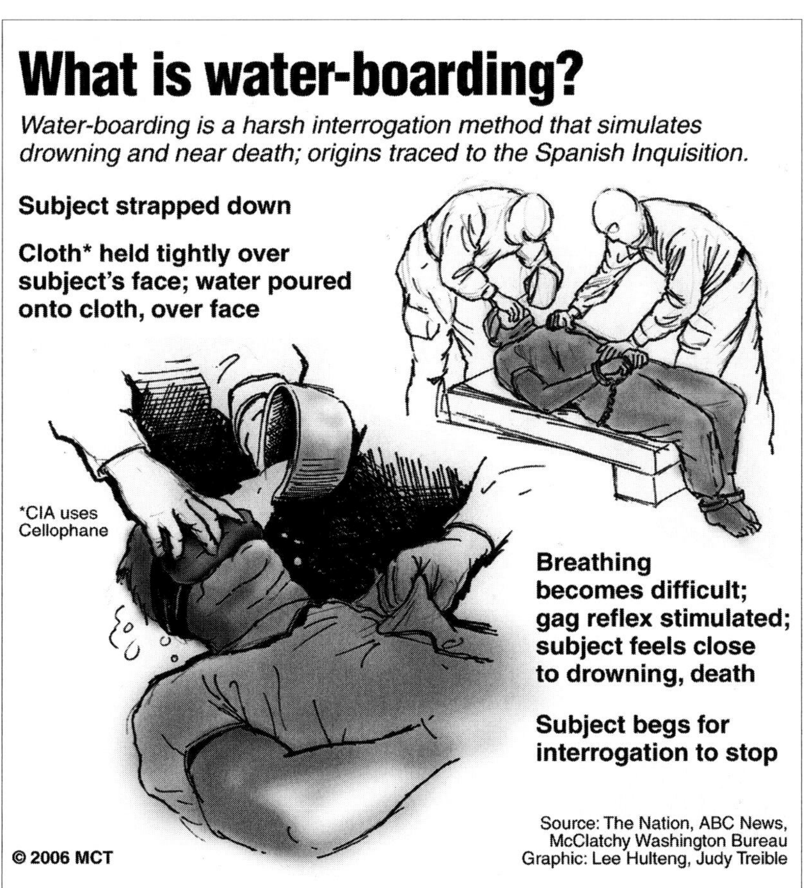

"ALL LIFE IS AN EXPERIMENT"

In April 1919, one of the acid bombs the terrorists tried to mail was intended for the Supreme Court justice Oliver Wendell Holmes. He was targeted for death, but that did not change his legal opinions. "All life," Holmes insisted, "is an experiment." There is no absolute certainty, as there is no perfect protection against dangerous enemies and destructive ideas. We do not silence views; rather, we let them battle for attention "in the competition of the market." And that requires Americans to "be eternally vigilant against attempts to check the expression of opinions that we loathe and believe to be fraught with death, unless they so imminently threaten immediate interference with the lawful and pressing purposes of the law that an immediate check is required to save the country."

A democracy must allow ideas to be aired, even loathsome ones that are "fraught with death." Those views flourish, or wither, as people hear them and weigh them against other views. This is indeed a very dangerous high-wire act requiring fine sensitivity and judgment. There is no guarantee the government will get it right. But all of life is an experiment. Otherwise, in the name of protecting democracy, we destroy it.

Justice Holmes got it exactly right: In America, we are living an experiment. That means there are no easy answers. Sometimes we will need to strike hard; sometimes we will need to pause. Fear paralyzes; democracy requires us to take a breath, to let the emotion subside, and to think. Our safety, our only safety, comes in that moment of agonizing weighing, and in our willingness to admit when we were terribly wrong. We have only imperfect safety, which is the glory of our nation: countries that demand perfect answers hide their mistakes in unmarked graves. There is an ebb and flow in the story of a nation—a time when loyalty and obedience are the highest virtues and another when dissent and doubt save us from ourselves. I hope *Master of Deceit* shows that we must always question both the heroes we favor and the enemies we hate. We must remain open-minded, even when the shadow of fear freezes our hearts.

Louis Post
1849–1928

Dr. Martin Luther King Jr.
1929–1968

Margaret Chase Smith
1897–1995

Frank Kameny
1925–2011

HOW I RESEARCHED AND WROTE THIS BOOK

Writing about the Cold War presents a unique set of challenges. In one way it is dusty and distant, especially for readers born after the fall of Soviet Communism. People, events, and issues that were of the greatest interest to older adults are invisible today—as out of sight and eclipsed as only the recent past can be. There is none of the romance and charm of the distant past, none of the current-events appeal of the latest disaster or triumph. And yet the Cold War is still controversial. The key issues it touches on—Communism, anti-Communism, government secrets, personal lies, the moral failings of our leaders, heterosexual and homosexual affairs—are still sensitive subjects. This is especially so because of the security decisions we need to make today. As I write this, Congress is holding hearings on the supposed radicalization of American Muslims that remind many of the HUAC hearings of the 1950s. So while one challenge is to bring a very obscure past to life, another is to negotiate through a charged field of political opinion. I hope this essay will help orient students and teachers who plan on doing their own research about this important period. At the end I've added a note about my own emotional experience in doing this research.

THE RESEARCH CHALLENGE

Books written in Hoover's lifetime were most often massaged by his PR staff. They make for lively reading but are slanted and incomplete. Books written in the 1970s, in the shadow of the Church Committee hearings, are often quite detailed and deeply critical. In the late 1980s and early 1990s came efforts to piece together all that was then known into narrative histories. The fall of Soviet Communism, the temporary opening of Soviet files, and then the release of the Venona decrypts in the '90s produced a new round of books that shaded old debates about, for example, Alger Hiss and Whittaker Chambers, in new ways. In the twenty-first century, we have started to have more specialized studies of various individuals and themes that take all the previous scholarship as a given background but offer new insight into one beat of the story.

As we came out of the Cold War, the weight of scholarship was on the left, often angrily so. The rise of modern conservatism has given rise both to defenses of Hoover and McCarthy and to a new interest in the enduring legacy of anti-Communism. And even as all this work has gone on in the academy and in serious adult books, Anthony Summers and his rumors (see pages 204–205) swept through popular culture and, falsely, defined Hoover in the general adult imagination. The one value of the Summers book is that it gathered all the rumors in one place so that they could be examined. That in turn has spawned a new round of (far less widely known) academic challenges and correctives to the Summers mythology.

As you can see, the field of researching and writing about Hoover and the Cold War is constantly shifting and changing. That makes for an exciting opportunity: take a small selection of books from different periods, line them up, and see how they treat similar events. That offers a quick, and powerful, lesson in the fact that who we are and the interests before us today influence what we see in the past. That does not mean the past is entirely invented and up to us to shape as we like. To be a historian, you must be fair to the evidence, willing to be proven wrong, and open to criticism. We may come to different conclusions, but we have to play by the same rules.

My own reading took place in several concentric phases. Before I even started to read about Hoover, I needed to get oriented in the story of Communism and anti-Communism. I knew, from my own childhood, that many of the key clashes of the period were still controversial. I began that phase of research with Ted Morgan's *Reds,* which is readable and fair-minded and covers the full arc of the period. A more detailed, scholarly, and generally pro-left view can be found in Ellen Schrecker's *Many Are the Crimes.* And Judy Kaplan and Linn Shapiro's *Red Diapers,* which Dr. Schrecker recommended to me, is fascinating. While other books discuss the great issues of Communism and anti-Communism as they shaped society, this book captures the family drama of living with radical beliefs. Having broadly mapped out the period, I could then enter the specific clashes. For example, for Hiss and Chambers, I used Allen Weinstein's *Perjury,* Sam Tanenhaus's *Whittaker Chambers,* and Weinstein and Alexander Vassiliev's *The Haunted Wood.*

My main guides to Hoover were *The Boss* by Athan G. Theoharis and John Stuart Cox and *Secrecy and Power* by Richard Gid Powers. *The Boss* is more dry and close to the sources but also ventures interesting psychological interpretations; *Secrecy and Power* is more expansive and interested in popular culture. *Broken,* also by Richard Powers, is a history of the FBI, not just Hoover, but it usefully draws on many of the themes of the earlier book. *J. Edgar Hoover: The Man and His Secrets* by Curt Gentry is good to use with the others, as it adds stories and is more recent, but it is less reliable. Ovid Demaris's collection of interviews, *J. Edgar Hoover: As They Knew Him,* is a real treasure trove for quotations but likely to be most useful for a student after he or she already knows the basic outline of Hoover's life.

For Hoover in the Palmer raid phase, my guide was Kenneth D. Ackerman's *Young J. Edgar.* For McCarthy, I used Schrecker's *Many Are the Crimes* for context and David M. Oshinsky's *A Conspiracy So Immense* for biography. *The Great Fear* by David Caute helped me to get a sense of the time and offered many useful anecdotes. David Garrow's book on the FBI and Dr. King was indispensable for making sense of the Hoover-King clash. David K. Johnson's *The Lavender Scare* deepened my understanding of the period in crucial ways. Late in my research, I came upon *J. Edgar Hoover and the Anti-interventionists* by Charles M. Douglas, as well as Rhodi Jeffreys-Jones's *The FBI: A History,* both of which added fresh perspectives I had not previously seen.

These books oriented me; they allowed me to feel comfortable in Hoover's life and to begin to know my way around. I offer additional comments in the source notes on the books I read most carefully. After doing this background work, I could read memoirs, go to websites, and read novels with some sense of context. I knew the world out of which they came. And that leads to the FBI files themselves.

Ever since Congress began investigating the FBI in the 1970s, a great many FBI files have been made available. Using the Freedom of Information Act, researchers have gained access to even more FBI material about specific individuals. Once I was oriented in the scholarship on Hoover and the Cold War, I began to go online to the FBI Freedom of Information site and to travel to the National Archives and Records Administration (NARA) in College Park, Maryland, to look at its collection of FBI photos and files. I loved my hours and days at NARA and hope to return. I did see Hoover afresh when looking at thousands of images of him and reading his phone logs and notes. He came alive to me as a person, beyond the issues and controversies.

Perhaps that is ultimately the difference between primary and secondary sources: secondary sources are like looking through binoculars as you focus the lenses. You are scanning the terrain and searching for guideposts. Primary sources are like the moment when you can see clearly through the lenses—the bird or bear or tree is suddenly crisp and sharp in its own individual color and personality. I was so pleased to have that aha! experience.

FEAR

This is a book about fear, and I was scared to write it. Really, I mean that. I grew up among the children of people who lost their jobs, or had to use false names, because of the Communist or socialist ideals they admired. My parents worked closely with some of those parents. One summer, my camp counselors were brothers whose parents were the Rosenbergs, the spies whose execution by our government is described in chapter 12. Even though today's FBI is not the organization it was under Hoover, after you read about the crimes committed by the Bureau, you can't help feeling some anxiety in exposing its dark past. And yet that is not the main reason I felt hesitant to write this book.

I was scared because I live in a world of liberals and leftists, in which there is tacit agreement to see Senator Joseph McCarthy and J. Edgar Hoover as terrible men and to speak passionately about the victims of their witch hunts. As you've seen, McCarthy was a reckless bully and opportunist who used people's fear. Hoover was the mastermind of an empire of secrets designed to terrify and silence anyone he disagreed with or disliked. Many did suffer because of them. Yet merely telling the story of their crimes and being self-righteous about their victims felt false to me. I knew that those on the left had their own secrets; their own liars, bullies, and opportunists. I felt scared to write this book because instead of joining in the chorus of the views I heard growing up, I would have to stand out and stand apart.

This book is filled with information that has never before been written about for teenagers, and that means I took risks. Some who admire Dr. King will be disturbed that I depict his moral failings. Those who believe it is important to encourage patriotism and respect for authority may think it is wrong of me to reveal the FBI's crimes. My frank discussion of the important role that rumors of homosexuality played in Hoover's day may bother both those who fear I am stigmatizing homosexuals as well as those who feel I am condoning activities they find morally objectionable. But this is the book I felt I needed to write; this is where the evidence I found led me. These are the truths about our past I felt teenagers deserve to know.

Have you had an experience similar to mine in writing this book, when your friends, your family, your teachers, all nod their heads about something, while you have doubts? It is hard to show that you don't really agree, you don't exactly fit in, especially when you see that kids who stand out get punished, especially if you have joined in on making fun of them. You know you are lying, but you don't want your friends, people you like, classmates you admire, to see you as a jerk, an unpopular fool, so you lie some more and grow more afraid of being found out.

In researching and writing this book, I learned to trust myself, to speak out even when everyone else seems to share an opposing view. Hoover silenced dissent both within the FBI and in American society. But so too did the Communist Party. The evil was never on one side; it was in silence.

THE WRITING CHALLENGE

Having gathered all this information, I faced the real problem: what to say? At every moment I had to weigh maintaining momentum versus pausing to tell a story. Everything was potentially interesting—from John Reed in Moscow to the Sacco and Vanzetti trials and protests; Langston Hughes's odyssey from Scottsboro through HUAC; the Abraham Lincoln Brigade in Spain and the way in which arguments over Communism and anti-Communism turned into neighborhood clashes between Jews and Catholics in American cities; the FBI's wartime successes and failures in Latin America; the Hollywood 10 hearings; the reactions of the children of famous reds to their parents; the Hiss-Chambers trials. But what belonged in this one book? What could give readers enough and not too much?

I wrote entries, from a few paragraphs to full chapters, on all the subjects I just listed but finally decided to leave them on the cutting-room floor. This is not meant to be a textbook; it cannot "cover" everything. I have tried to hone the story down to one that moves along but says enough to engage readers. Finding that link to readers was another challenge. I tried out innumerable first chapters—from a vivid description of 9/11 and the fear it created, based on one of my neighbor's personal experiences in being at the towers as they were collapsing, to finally the Dr. King letter I have now. I particularly liked my 9/11 chapter but came to feel that those events themselves have become history, while the unfamiliar example of the FBI plot was a better lead into the dark story that would follow.

The truth is, I could not tell which beats in the story belonged until I tried my hand at all of them. If there is a lesson in that for students, it is that it is OK to be excessive, to do too much. Why would I do that? you may ask. Well, because when you are full of your research, you probably don't know what is most important or what will communicate your ideas in the most effective way. Better to get it all down. Then, once you have your full story on paper, you can prune. Just remember that, as they say in fiction, you will have to "kill your darlings"—let go of bits that you like but that are getting in the way of your larger goal: sharing with readers the fascinating information you have discovered and the insights you have to offer.

NOTES

Prologue: Blackmail

p. viii: "King, there is only one thing . . . bared to the nation": quoted in Garrow, 125–126. This pathbreaking book not only reveals the FBI's campaign against Dr. King but also carefully weighs the possible explanations for it. Garrow went on to write a Pulitzer Prize–winning book about Dr. King called *Bearing the Cross: Martin Luther King, Jr., and the Southern Christian Leadership Conference* (New York: Morrow, 1986).

p. viii: King believed the note was telling him to commit suicide: U.S. Senate, *Final Report of the Select Committee to Study Government Operations with Respect to Intelligence Activities, Book III: Supplementary Detailed Staff Reports on Intelligence Activities and the Rights of Americans,* 94th Congress, 2nd sess., 1976, pp. 159–160, Mary Ferrell Foundation website, http://www.maryferrell.org/mffweb/archive/viewer/showDoc.do?docId=1159&relPageId=165. This is the report of the Church Committee, charged with investigating the FBI's illegal activities. Andrew Young, a close aide to King, told the committee, "I think that the disturbing thing to Martin was that he felt somebody was trying to get him to commit suicide, and because it was a tape of a meeting in Washington and the postmark was from Florida, we assumed nobody had the capacity to do that other than the Federal Bureau of Investigation." Young testified that both he and Ralph Abernathy, who also heard the tape and read the letter, interpreted it as inviting Dr. King to take his own life.

Part One: Nothing in This Book Matters Until You Care about Communism

Chapter One: John Reed and Revolution

p. 4: To see how the full arc of American history would look if written from this first point of view, see the best-selling *A Patriot's History of the United States,* by Larry Schweikart and Michael Allen (New York: Sentinel, 2004).

p. 4: To see how the full arc of American history would look if written from this second point of view, see the best-selling *A People's History of the United States,* by Howard Zinn (New York: New Press, 1997).

p. 4: "Nothing teaches . . . organized on a grand scale": John Reed, "Bolshevism in America," *Revolutionary Age,* December 18, 1918, Early American Marxism website, http://www.marxisthistory.org/history/usa/parties/spusa/1918/1218=reed=bolshinamerica.pdf.

p. 5: "New light seems to pour . . . at one stroke": Crossman, 23. Published in 1950, this collection gave former Communists an opportunity to describe why they had once believed in Marxism and why their views had changed. The book is an excellent resource for anyone interested in the power, and the failure, of Communism, which is a crucial theme for the entire history of the twentieth century.

p. 6: According to a recent survey . . . how to teach evolution: Nicholas Bakalar, "On Evolution, Biology Teachers Stray from Lesson Plan," *New York Times,* February 7, 2011.

p. 8: "we who were strong in love! . . . was very heaven!" William Wordsworth, "The Prelude." Although they are written in a poetic voice that takes some effort to make out, Wordsworth's lines really do capture what it is to be young at a revolutionary moment—with a hint of how you view that golden enthusiasm when you look back on it later.

pp. 8–9: "The tree of liberty . . . patriots and tyrants": Thomas Jefferson letter to William Smith, November 13, 1787 (widely available online).

p. 9: "shall grow weary . . . overthrow it": Lincoln's first inaugural address (widely available online). American Communists often cited both Jefferson's and Lincoln's lines, especially in the mid-1930s, when they were stressing how all-American they were.

p. 10: "suddenly realized . . . a glory to die": Reed, 257–259.

p. 10: "A great idea has triumphed": quoted in Reed, 309.

Chapter Two: The Rise of J. Edgar Hoover: The First Secret

p. 11: " 'wild' and 'crazy' and 'irresponsible' ": quoted in Max Eastman, "John Reed, Bolshevik Envoy to the United States—A Character Sketch," *The Evening Call,* February 3, 1918, Early American Marxism website, http://www.marxisthistory.org/subject/usa/eam/index.html.

Eastman was, at the time, a big fan of Reed's and was citing these negative terms as coming from weak, conventional people.

p. 11: "Christian nations," quoted in Powers, *Secrecy and Power,* 29. One of the shining strengths of Powers's book is how he blends his reading of the surviving scraps of Hoover's childhood writing with a broader look at the world in which Hoover grew up. Powers is as unsparing in his consideration of evidence as Theoharis and Cox are in *The Boss,* but Powers is somewhat more willing to consider or credit what Hoover's own views might have been. Powers is also interested in media and popular culture as well as in Hoover and the FBI, which adds an extra dimension to his treatment.

p. 12: "the saddest moment of the year . . . part of my life": quoted in Gentry, 66. The line seems like something anyone might have written, but in view of how much Hoover's life was later built around small circles of men bonded in secret activities, it suggests a stronger feeling than the usual platitude.

Theoharis and Cox, in *The Boss,* posit that working in a male secret society was central to Hoover and helped him deal with his inner conflicts. Their book is a careful study of Hoover based on close reading of FBI documents. It is drier and more narrowly focused than the Powers book but is an essential resource that anyone who researches Hoover must use. I personally felt more drawn to their psychological reading of Hoover than the more broadly social-cultural one used by Powers.

Gentry's is an engaging book; he is a journalist who is a good writer and did extensive research. As I compared it with Powers' and with Theoharis and Cox's, though, I felt it too easily broadcast rumor as fact and is not as reliable as the other two. It is a good read and offers many useful and juicy quotations, but its interpretations need to be checked against other sources.

p. 14: "a very forceful kind of person," "made herself felt," "always expected that J.E. was going to be successful," "pushed," "as much as she could," "ran a beautiful home for him," and "very strong personalities": quoted in Demaris, 5–6. Every subsequent author has used Demaris's interviews as the basis for describing Hoover's relationship with his mother.

p. 14: "the only person . . . abiding affection": quoted in Purvis, 61.

Chapter Three: "There Will Have to Be Bloodshed"

p. 18: "We have been dreaming . . . tyrannical institutions": quoted in Ackerman, 15. This book is readable and informative and captures this early phase of Hoover's career better than any other work I've seen. Any student or teacher who wants to focus on the Palmer raids should use it.

p. 20: "American Workingmen" and "A successful revolution . . . invincible": Nikolai Lenin, "A Letter to American Workingmen," *The Liberator,* vol. 1, no. 11 (January 1919), 8, Marxists Internet Archive, http://marxists.anu.edu.au/history/usa/culture/pubs/liberator/index.htm. The entire issue of the *Liberator* with Lenin's letter is viewable here. I found looking at the ads, books reviews, and other articles helpful. It gave me a sense of the world in which readers would have found the speech—the bookstores and tearooms where radicals gathered in New York.

p. 21: "Palmer . . . in this country": quoted in Ackerman, 25.

pp. 22–23: "make a study of subversive activities" and "what action . . . prosecution": ibid., 64.

Chapter Four: "We're Going Back to Russia—That's a Free Country"

p. 27: "We're going back to Russia—that's a free country": ibid., 117. For a fuller depiction of the raid and its aftermath, see Ackerman, 113–119. I also used Finan, 1–2, and the National Popular Government League report of 1920, which he cites. You can find that report, which makes for fascinating reading, at the Internet Archive, http://www.archive.org/details/toamericanpeople00natiuoft.

For a broader background on Communism and anti-Communism in the period of the raids, see Morgan, 54–87. This readable survey traces the history of Communism in America, Communist spying, and anti-Communism throughout the period covered in this book. I found it very useful as a background book to consult. High-school students doing reports should use its index to orient themselves to key players and issues.

p. 28: "convert small strikes . . . we must be merciless": quoted in Ackerman, 121–122.

Chapter Five: Legal Rights: Hoover vs. Louis Post

p. 31: traveled to South Carolina in 1871 to gather evidence against the Ku Klux Klan: Post is discussed in Ackerman, but I found the interesting detail about his early role working against the Klan in Jeffreys-Jones, 23. This is a readable, recent survey of FBI history that is a useful survey for a high-school student. The tone is less labored than some, less angry than others, which makes it all the more useful.

p. 33: "The Bully Bolshevik," "disrespectfully dedicated . . . Post," and "The 'Reds' at Ellis Island . . . land of the brave": quoted in Ackerman, 274–276.

Part Two: The War of Images

Chapter Six: Clyde: The Second Secret

p. 37: "stocks have reached . . . plateau": quoted in Robert Brent Toplin, "The Parallel with 1929 We Ignore at Our Peril," History News Network, September 23, 2008, http://hnn.us/articles/54824.html.

p. 41: "The tougher the attacks get, the tougher I get": quoted in Powers, *Secrecy and Power,* 474.

p. 41: J. Edgar Hoover was a real-life Sherlock Holmes . . . nation safe: ibid., 167.

p. 41: "looks utterly unlike . . . mincing step": quoted in Gentry, 159.

pp. 41–44: The question of Hoover's possible homosexuality, especially his extremely close relationship with Clyde Tolson, is explored by any author who writes about him. The first two rumors were given wide currency by Anthony Summers, a British hack author of gossip-filled celebrity bios. Despite his dubious credentials, the stories were so widely shared that they are now taken by many nonexperts as absolute truth. Nearly every adult I spoke with about this book began by asking about Hoover's supposed cross-dressing. I suspect there is an element of vengeance in people's desire to believe such unlikely tales — the relentless inquisitor turns out to have a closet full of secrets. In *J. Edgar Hoover, Sex, and Crime,* Theoharis, who has studied Hoover's files in the most scholarly detail and is one of his most severe critics, examines each of the Summers myths and demolishes them. In *The Lavender Scare,* David Johnson points out that the orgy rumor is "clearly a homophobic fantasy" (page 11). These tales should be laid to rest.

Of course we can ultimately only surmise what happened in private between Hoover and Tolson. Hoover's lifetime secretary destroyed his confidential files, and no historian has reported finding Tolson's papers. Unless some new evidence suddenly appears, we are left to rely on best guesses. In *Secrecy and Power,* Powers describes Hoover and Tolson as life partners on the emotional level, but that is as far as he can be certain. He is the one who found the photo of the sleeping Tolson. I found the shot of reclining Tolson in the FBI NARA file. In *The Boss,* Theoharis and Cox postulate that Hoover was so repressed, so focused on his work, and so attached to his clusters of male friends that he did not need further intimacy. To me this image of a man whose defense was against himself is more compelling than seeing him as a person who was hiding his actions from others.

p. 42: "homosocial": Rosswurm, 30. Rosswurm uses the term within a longer discussion of Hoover's childhood and personality that is quite useful, though certainly written for an academic audience.

p. 43: "I have always held girls . . . for my actions": quoted in Ackerman, 321.

pp. 43–44: Hoover's fears: Theoharis and Cox, 47. In that book's acknowledgments, the authors thank Michael Sheard, a Yale psychiatrist, and his wife, Wendy Stedman Sheard, for comments and for guiding them to relevant psychological literature which they used in the text.

p. 43: "electrocute" and the description of the air-filtration system: Gentry, 462.

p. 44: "the boss don't understand . . . death of them": ibid., 280.

p. 44: "compact body . . . virile humanity": ibid., 159.

Chapter Seven: Public Enemy Number One: John Dillinger

p. 48: "My conscience . . . stole from the people": ibid., 167.

p. 50: "John Herbert Dillinger . . . July, 1934": Whitehead, 103. Whitehead was a prize-winning journalist, and the book is an easy read. However, in light of what we now know, it is as interesting for what it doesn't say, or how it spins the stories it tells, as for actual information about the FBI.

p. 50: "a challenge to law and order and civilization itself": quoted in Gentry, 168.

pp. 50–56: Any book on Hoover written since the 1970s includes the Purvis story. More recently, Purvis's son cowrote a book-length indictment of Hoover's treatment of his father; I mined it for useful quotations and rich descriptions about the run-up to the Little Bohemia raid (Purvis, 95–96) and the disastrous raid itself (110).

p. 51: "fever for action": Purvis, 97.

p. 51: "Halt!" "We're federal officers!" and "Stop the car": ibid., 110.

p. 52: "stay on Dillinger. Go anywhere the trail takes you": quoted in Whitehead, 104.

p. 52: "who was pacing the library . . . Washington," "darted toward an alley . . . pocket," and "Slugs tore into . . . chase was over": ibid., 105–106.

p. 54: "OK, Johnnie, drop your gun": quoted in Powers, *Broken,* 153. This more recent book by Powers incorporates much of the story told in *Secrecy and Power* but extends it beyond Hoover's day.

p. 54: "One man alone is responsible . . . Hoover": quoted in Purvis, 185.

p. 54: "Mr. Purvis is also . . . on the publicity there": ibid., 189–190.

p. 54: "our system of operations . . . a case is broken": ibid., 235.

p. 54: "so-called 'hero' of a situation": ibid., 247.

p. 55: "If it's the last thing I do . . . dead or alive": ibid., 260. While I found these quotations in Purvis's book, the description of the Hoover-Purvis conflict is in line with the reliable analysis in Powers, *Secrecy and Power,* 224–226.

p. 55: "he is not to come to the office": quoted in Powers, *Secrecy and Power,* 263.

p. 55: "inside story . . . man-hunting organization": Purvis, 281.

p. 59: "closerthanthis," "slight case of merger," "infanticipating," "the Mister and Miseries," "sharing separate teepees," and "Good evening . . . ships at sea": quoted in Gabler, 267. This is an intelligent, deeply researched, fascinating book. It is long, and diligently covers all of Winchell's life, so students and teachers are more likely to dip into it than read it through. The citations are nearly impossible to make out, as the relevant page is stacked amid so much other type that the reader constantly gets lost. Still, it is a necessary resource for anyone researching the growth of the media and the power of celebrity culture, subjects that should be of interest to many high-school students.

p. 60: "found out his favorite drink . . . about everybody": ibid., 187. The Stork Club is another subject that would make for terrific student research; the ancestor of modern "hot" clubs guarded by velvet ropes, it offers a window into a different time and place that links to our own obsessions. As a starting point, Gabler's book offers a mini-history of the club. There are also a number of websites devoted to it.

p. 61: "See Uncle Sam . . . march on crime": quoted in Powers, *Secrecy and Power,* 162.

Chapter Eight: The Crisis of Capitalism: The Third Secret

p. 66: "At the very moment . . . showed striking gains": *Proletarian Literature in the United States.* I found this book both disturbing and fascinating reading. Looking back from the twenty-first century, I found the insistence of what art needs to be quite alien. On the other hand, the assumption of how cultured and widely read in European literature any artist would be is also striking. An alert high-school student interested in the rules we set for art—whether the assumptions we have today or those of the past—will find much to discover in Joseph Freeman's introductory essay, from which the quotation is taken.

pp. 67–68: The largely unknown story of the Americans who immigrated to the Soviet Union during the Depression and their grim fate is retold in Tzouliadis. This is a useful resource for any motivated student who wants to explore the subject. For the Abolins' trip to Russia, the school, and baseball, see pages 17–19.

p. 68: examples of Communist front organizations: Morgan, 167–172.

pp. 68–69: American Communist Party membership numbers: Schrecker, *McCarthyism,* 11 and 15.

p. 69: "an enslaved and oppressed people": "Minutes of the Second Congress of the Communist International," Fourth Session, July 25, Marxists Internet Archive, http://www.marxists.org/history/international/comintern/2nd-congress/ch04.htm#v1-p121.

p. 70: "Negro Moses": quoted in O'Reilly, 14. Any student or teacher interested in exploring the FBI's involvement with civil rights, black nationalism, and black communities can use this book as a resource. See also Powers, *Secrecy and Power,* 128.

p. 70: "The colored people . . . if they had the opportunity": quoted in Powers, *Secrecy and Power,* 411.

p. 70: The story of the Hoover family possibly being partially African American comes from Millie McGhee, *Secrets Uncovered* (Havre De Grace, MD: Allen-Morris, 2002), and is cited in Ackerman, 5 and 42. It is easy to find summaries of McGhee's argument on the Internet. The problem is that she is relying not only on family oral history—which may well be true but needs confirmation—but also on memories of her own that she claims to have blocked and then recovered through therapy. This is very treacherous territory where fantasy, mythology, and fact can easily blur. Ackerman cites a genealogist who does not think her case is convincing.

p. 74: For information on the Scottsboro case, see James Goodman. This book is a treat in-the-waiting for any serious AP American history teacher or student. An example of modern history writing, it retells the full story of the Scottsboro case and also explores the different ways each beat in the trials was framed, explained, told, and retold by the many communities who had a stake in the outcome. Thus it is as much about many segments of America as it is about the fate of the nine young men. For basic facts about the case, see Douglas O. Linder, "Famous American Trials: The 'Scottsboro Boys' Trials, 1931–1937," University of Missouri–Kansas City School of Law website, http://www.law2.umkc.edu/faculty/projects/ftrials/scottsboro.

p. 75: "overwhelming drama of moral struggle" and Wright's conversion to Communism: Crossman, 155. This is a vivid, wonderfully written book that makes an engaging source for any student or teacher interested in such subjects as the Depression, Communism, writing, black writers, or the life of Richard Wright.

p. 76: Hoover on Scottsboro: O'Reilly, 17–18.

p. 76: "isolated each artist . . . and go mad" and "the revolution . . . mass-meeting": quoted in *Proletarian Literature in the United States,* introduction.

p. 76: "You are either pioneers . . . will mould you" and "You will be indescribably crushed . . . total destruction": quoted in Tanenhaus, 75. The editorial writer was Whittaker Chambers, who appears later in the book under the pseudonym Carl. Chambers is a seemingly unlikely subject for a biography, since to an earlier generation of writers he was the villain, or at best a dupe, in a central trial of the postwar era. But in carefully sorting through his life and writing, Tanenhaus gives a sense of the crosscurrents of the Cold War. The book was useful to me both in taking me through one person's journey in and out of Communism and in taking conservatism—which is so much a part of our political landscape now—seriously. Any motivated student who is writing about the Cold War in America, Communist spying, or the flashpoint conflicts of the time needs to make use of this book.

pp. 78–79: "Get out of our ranks!" "I-It's May Day . . . to march," "Get out," "hands lifted me . . . flowed past me," and "they're blind": Crossman, 160–161.

Part Three: The Turning Point: Subversive Activities

Chapter Nine: The Secret Assignment

pp. 83–84: the coup plot: Gentry, 201–206.

pp. 84–85: the Texas group and the "Jew Deal": Burrough, 131. This book is an easy introduction to the history of Texas oil money, which played an important part in the Hoover story. It's an entertaining read and a good place to start if you want to research that strand in American history. A student interested in looking at energy policy—using that current issue as a lens for understanding U.S. and world history—could do well to use Daniel Yergin's *The Prize: The Epic Quest for Oil, Money, and Power* (New York: Simon & Schuster, 1991) (also a PBS series, available on DVD) along with Burrough to get oriented.

p. 85: "If you wore . . . not get arrested": quoted in Morgan, 149.

p. 85: "subversive activities in the United States" and "any matters referred to it by the Department of State": Theoharis and Cox, 150–151; Gentry, 207; Powers, *Secrecy and Power,* 229.

pp. 85–87: The story of FDR's request and Hoover's response, as well as the matter of Hoover's filing system, is covered in every recent biography.

p. 85: "be handled quite confidentially . . . aware of this request": quoted in Theoharis, *Abuse of Power,* 4. The result of a lifetime's work reading and analyzing Hoover-era files from the FBI, this book by a master historian is necessary reading for any teacher who wants deeper understanding of the story I tell in this book.

p. 87: "broad enough to cover any expansion" and "intelligence and counter-espionage work": quoted in Theoharis and Cox, 176.

pp. 87–88: The story of Hoover's efforts to please FDR by gathering information about Lindbergh and the anti-interventionists was news to me and made fascinating reading. It is summarized in Jeffreys-Jones, 126–127, and forms the heart of Douglas M. Charles's *J. Edgar Hoover and the Anti-interventionists.*

p. 88: the FBI's dance around the logbook rules on wiretapping: Charles, 50–51.

p. 89: "appreciation" and "for the many interesting . . . have made to me": ibid., 59.

p. 89: "on every member of Congress . . . the Senate": quoted in Theoharis and Cox, 308.

p. 89: "black-bag job": Gentry, 283. For a summary of illegal FBI interception activities, see Gentry, 281–283.

p. 89: Do Not File: Charles, 52.

p. 90: Hoover and the America First Committee: ibid., 62.

p. 93: effects of his mother's death on Hoover: Powers, *Secrecy and Power,* 259–260.

p. 93: "Hoover's capacity to feel deeply for other human beings": Purvis, 61.

p. 93: For a wonderful essay that explores the psychology of the "fellow travelers" in a Communist regime, see Tony Judt, "Captive Minds," *New York Review of Books,* September 30, 2010, http://www.nybooks.com/articles/archives/2010/sep/30/captive-minds/.

Part Four: The Fighting War

pp. 94–95: Information on the forced famine in the Ukraine and the Battle of Stalingrad is easily available online. Scholars still debate whether Stalin's aim was the deliberate mass murder of Ukrainians or whether his main goal was to industrialize, with the famine deaths a price he did not mind paying. Was he totally heartless or actually genocidal? Similarly, there are debates over whether the Holocaust was a unique case because Hitler's aim was the eradication of one ethnic group, while Stalin was inflicting a brutal economic policy aimed at eliminating a class of relatively wealthy farmers. These are powerful and troubling questions motivated students can explore. I found this short essay particularly compelling: Timothy Snyder, "Hitler vs. Stalin: Who Killed More?" *New York Review of Books,* March 10, 2011, http://www.nybooks.com/articles/archives/2011/mar/10/hitler-vs-stalin-who-killed-more/.

The story of Stalin's crimes has only recently begun to be told in books for younger readers. Two 2011 novels, Ruta Sepetys's *Between Shades of Gray* (New York: Philomel, 2011) and Eugene Yelchin's *Breaking Stalin's Nose* (New York: Holt, 2011), began to correct this absence. Both belong in any classroom that deals with twentieth-century history.

Chapter Ten: Great Injustice

p. 97: "enemies of the working class" and "grind them down . . . without flagging": quoted in Tzouliadis, 81.

p. 97: "We shall annihilate . . . families and relatives": ibid., 94.

p. 98: Young Communists competed to expose enemies of the state: ibid., 82–83.

p. 99: the fate of the Abolin family: ibid., 101.

p. 99: Paul Robeson's repertoire: *The Odyssey of Paul Robeson,* Omega Classics (OCD 3007), coproduced by Paul Robeson Jr., contains all these songs and more and is my personal favorite.

pp. 99–100: "We all knew . . . said a word" and "Sometimes great injustices . . . just cause": quoted in Tzouliadis, 98.

Chapter Eleven: Hoover's War

pp. 103–105: The Nazi sub story as Hoover wanted it told can be found in Whitehead, 202–203. For a telling of the events by the FBI today, see "George John Dasch and the Nazi Saboteurs," at the FBI website, http://www.fbi.gov/about-us/history/famous-cases/nazi-saboteurs. Gentry, 288–289, has Dasch's version.

p. 103: "How old are you? . . . a good time": quoted in Whitehead, 202.

p. 103: "in their hearts . . . oozing away": ibid., 203.

p. 104: "Yesterday Napoleon called" and "seized the suitcase . . . on the desk": quoted in Gentry, 289.

p. 104: "FBI Captures . . . Landed by Subs": ibid., 291.

p. 106: "German, Italian, and Communist sympathies": quoted in Powers, *Broken,* 173.

p. 107: "I thought the army was getting a bit hysterical" and "one efficient method . . . consideration": quoted in Powers, *Secrecy and Power,* 249.

p. 107: "We must clean up democracy . . . from abroad": ibid., 258.

p. 107: "the Communist virus": ibid., 261.

Part Five: The War of Shadows

Chapter Twelve: The Hope of the World

p. 111: code-named Enormous: Haynes, Klehr, and Vassiliev, 34. Alert readers will notice that Alexander Vassiliev is also the coauthor of Allen Weinstein's *The Haunted Wood.* Vassiliev was a former KBG agent who brought out evidence of Soviet spying after the fall of Communism. Years later, he claimed that he had filled a notebook with more information but that the notebook had not been available to him when he worked on the first book.

Many aspects of this story raise concerns: Did he really keep the notebook back in the Soviet Union? We cannot check it against the now once again largely closed Russian files. How did he manage to get it out? Were his notes, if real, accurate? Even if the notes were real and accurate, since the Soviet files are closed, we have no way to check his information against other sources. We know from experience that secret agencies like the KGB and the FBI used deception even within their own internal filing systems.

So this is a book about which many reasonable questions may be asked. And yet, taken together with the Venona decryptions and the general body of evidence, the picture Vassiliev paints of more extensive Soviet spying, actively aided by the American Communist Party, is plausible. Interested researchers should consult this book but look to other sources, as well as online reviews and discussions, to evaluate what they find in it.

p. 111: "the crime of the century," quoted in Powers, *Secrecy and Power,* 303.

p. 113: "how she felt . . . convictions go" and "replied without hesitation . . . deepest admiration": quoted in Haynes, Klehr, and Vassiliev, 105.

p. 114: "proceed against other individuals" and "Proceedings against his wife . . . this matter": quoted in Powers, *Secrecy and Power,* 303–304.

p. 115: "worse than murder" and "Millions more . . . your treason": ibid., 302.

pp. 115–116: "a tremendous crowd . . . screamed at us" and "silently faced . . . shrieked with joy": quoted in Kaplan and Shapiro, 86.

p. 117: the FBI in the media and popular culture: Powers, *Secrecy and Power,* 255.

Chapter Thirteen: Tailgunner Joe

p. 118: "like a mongrel dog . . . bite your leg off": Senator Paul Douglas quoted in Oshinsky, 15.

p. 119: "The Democratic Christian world" and "The reason why we find . . . we can give": quoted in Oshinsky, 108. Oshinsky's book is the best serious biography of McCarthy by an established historian; anyone researching the senator should be aware of it as a reference. James Cross Giblin has made McCarthy's story more accessible for young readers in his *The Rise and Fall of Senator Joe McCarthy* (New York: Clarion, 2009). I was aware that he was working on that book as I began to write this one; I hope readers find our two quite different books a useful pair.

p. 119: "as the only man who . . . inside one as well": ibid., 7.

p. 119: a list of 205 people: ibid., 109.

p. 120: "The FBI kept Joe McCarthy . . . all we had": quoted in Theoharis and Cox, 283, footnote 2.

pp. 120–121: the anti-homosexual strand in the period of the Red Scare: Johnson. This book is an important academic study that adds an otherwise missing dimension to our understanding of the period.

p. 120: Ninety-one of these employees lost their jobs: ibid., 17.

p. 121: A national survey . . . at least one homosexual experience: "Prevalence of Homosexuality: Brief Summary of U.S. Studies," The Kinsey Institute for Research in Sex, Gender, and Reproduction website, http://www.iub.edu/~kinsey/resources/bibhomoprev.html.

pp. 121–122: "I have instructed . . . to defend himself": quoted in Caute, 106. This book was recommended to me by a historian who recalled that it had given him a vivid sense of the Age of Fear McCarthy did so much to create. It is an excellent resource for the stories of lives harmed by the anti-Communist purges. The book is written to expose the damage caused by McCarthy and others, and you can feel the author's anger. You might pair it with a book like Haynes, Klehr, and Vassiliev's *Spies,* which focuses on the actual Soviet plots.

p. 122: "fraud": quoted in Oshinsky, 175.

p. 122: "You will find out who . . . to do about it?": ibid., 171.

p. 122: Money secretly contributed by Texas oilmen covered the costs of distributing the doctored photo far and wide: Burrough, 223, footnote 1.

p. 123: "You're a real SOB. . . . dirty work": Senator John Bricker quoted in Oshinsky, 132.

p. 123: "dig out and destroy" and "It was a dirty, foul . . . next to them in church": quoted in Caute, 48.

p. 123: "Some people have told me . . . like gentlemen": quoted in Oshinsky, 394–395.

p. 124: "The American people are sick and tired . . . used to be in America" and "The right to criticize . . . thought control would have set in": Margaret Chase, "Declaration of Conscience," Margaret Chase Library website, Northwood University, http://www.mcslibrary.org/program/library/declaration.htm.

pp. 125–127: The Venona Project is discussed in any adult or academic book on Communism and/or anti-Communism in this period published since the mid-1990s. To see the actual coded messages and decryptions and learn more about the project, see "Venona: Soviet Espionage and the American Response, 1939–1957," Central Intelligence Agency website, https://www.cia.gov/library/center-for-the-study-of-intelligence/csi-publications/books-and-monographs/venona-soviet-espionage-and-the-american-response-1939–1957/venona.htm. Scholars who have their doubts about the value of the Venona material point out that a person's being named by a Soviet spy does not necessarily mean that that person actually helped the Communists.

p. 127: "auxiliary service to Soviet intelligence": Haynes, Klehr, and Vassiliev, 548.

p. 129: "perhaps the most significant intelligence loss in U.S. history": quoted in Weiner, 158. This is a lengthy, detailed, but compelling book that any teacher or student interested in the CIA and spycraft must at least consult.

p. 129: "There are today . . . death for society": quoted in Theoharis and Cox, 257.

Part Six: The Age of Fear

Chapter Fourteen: Loyalty

p. 133: "best and happiest years": Attorney General William Rogers quoted in Powers, *Secrecy and Power,* 313.

pp. 134–135: Murchison's covering of the almost $20,000 bill: Burrough, 227.

p. 135: the ice-cream incident: Ungar, 272.

p. 136: "is a former Marine . . . he so views me," "attack subversives," and "But sometimes a knock is a boost": quoted in Gentry, 431.

p. 136: "benign" and "barbaric": quoted in Fast, 224. A friend told me that his father kept books on Marx covered with brown paper in this period. In fact if you ask anyone who lived in a left-leaning family at this time, they have similar stories. A sense of the fearfulness of the time can also be gained from Caute and from Kaplan and Shapiro.

p. 136: By 1954, 52 percent of Americans . . . lose their citizenship: Caute, 215.

p. 137: "you maintained in your library . . Marxism": quoted in Caute, 280.

p. 137: "handshake had to be firm . . . crucial handclasp," "immaculate appearance," and "complete control": Felt and O'Connor, 1–2. This memoir was published at the end of Felt's life for reasons that alert readers may have already picked up and others will learn at the end of this book. It gives a personal insider's view of Hoover's FBI by an agent who was loyal to the director but even more so to his sense of honor in service. For more on Hoover's rules — official and unofficial — see Theoharis and Cox, 104.

p. 138: "their clothing style . . . clumsy manners": quoted in Weinstein and Vassiliev, 276.

p. 139: "he was always talking about world peace" and "saw a map of Russia": quoted in Caute, 215.

p. 139: "he would never wear . . . not a capitalist": ibid., 278. Caute's book is a great source for examples of how the loyalty system turned fear, prejudice, gossip, and sometimes envy or greed into accusation.

p. 139: But she chose to join her parents, who were teaching at a college in America: The college referred to is Black Mountain College, which made a home for many European artists escaping from the Nazis and was not at all sympathetic to McCarthyism. It no longer exists, but any student interested in researching a troubled yet fascinating school where European modern art met American idealism should look it up.

p. 140: "They were afraid. Everyone was afraid" and "There were agents . . . Terrible": quoted in Kaplan and Shapiro, 131.

p. 140: "J. Edgar Hoover had sent . . . instructions of J. Edgar Hoover": quoted in Fast, 288.

p. 141: "Of course the fact that . . . doesn't it?": quoted in Caute, 168.

p. 141: "My impression was . . . differed on that": ibid., 278.

p. 141: How to Spot a Communist: ibid., 296. The guide was withdrawn a week after it was published, but it clearly reflected the beliefs and prejudices that shaped decisions within the army.

p. 141: "security risk": ibid., 273. See also Johnson.

p. 141: Of the 654 people who were forced to leave . . . to be homosexual: Timothy Naftali, "Alger Hiss and the Chambers' Secrets," paper given at NYU Center for the United States and the Cold War, Alger Hiss and History Conference, April 5, 2007.

p. 142: "There can be no proof . . . susceptible to proof": R. W. Scott McLeod, "American Political Democracy and the Problem of Personnel Security," *Department of State Bulletin,* vol. 33, no. 849 (October 3, 1955), 572, Internet Archives website, http://www.archive.org/stream/departmentofstate3355unit/departmentofstate3355unit_djvu.txt.

p. 142: The film *Advise and Consent* is discussed in Johnson, 135.

p. 142: They would stage a seemingly compromising encounter: ibid., 111.

p. 142: "much as the FBI . . . destroying itself": Fast, 330.

p. 142: Conservatives claimed that both the United States government and United Nations were filled with unmanly pencil pushers: Johnson, 90–97.

p. 144: "his look of supreme . . . frightening": Patricia Bosworth's mother quoted in Bosworth, 240. This book provides an insightful woman's view of Hoover.

p. 145: "Don't present me with the choice . . . to be an informer" and "It seems to me . . . this kind of choice": "HUAC Hearings on Communist Infiltration of the Motion-Picture Industry, 1951–1952," Digital History website, http://www.digitalhistory.uh.edu/historyonline/huac_infiltration2.cfm.

Parks's powerful statement can be found in many histories of this period. Anyone interested in film history who wants to know more about the blacklist and its influence on Hollywood might begin by consulting Paul Buhle and Dave Wagner's *Blacklisted: The Film Lover's Guide to the Hollywood Blacklist* (New York: Palgrave Macmillan, 2003) and then watching some of the movies it discusses.

p. 146: "I remember a sense of silence . . . hours and hours": quoted in Caute, 513.

p. 147: "a degradation ceremony": Kazan, 447.

p. 147: "the Party fellows get away with . . . contrary convictions": ibid., 457.

p. 148: "I could not use the name of another person and bring trouble on him": quoted in Walter Goodman, 413.

p. 148: "I was experiencing a bitterness . . . to humiliate himself?": Miller, 334. For more about the Kazan-Miller story and how it relates to *The Crucible,* see the epilogue to my book *Witch-Hunt: Mysteries of the Salem Witch Trials.*

Chapter Fifteen: No Decency

p. 149: "situation of fear" and the 10–1 ratio of calls: Oshinsky, 399, and Morgan, 477.

p. 151: "Until this moment, Senator . . . your recklessness": quoted in Oshinsky, 462.

p. 151: "Let us not assassinate . . . no sense of decency?": ibid., 463. The 1964 documentary *Point of Order* (also issued as a book) is well worth seeing to get the full flavor of this intense moment.

pp. 151–152: "They know exactly where to throw . . . to commit murder": ibid., 466.

pp. 152–153: In January 1954, half of Americans polled . . . 45 percent disliked him: ibid., 464.

p. 153: "hate, fear, and suspicion" and "a handful of prodigiously wealthy men": quoted in Burrough, 233.

Part Seven: The Land of Lies

p. 154: Hoover and the Kennedy assassination: Powers, *Secrecy and Power,* 383–390.

p. 154: A recent biography of Malcolm X: Manning Marable, *Malcolm X: A Life of Reinvention* (New York: Viking, 2011).

p. 154: the FBI settlement in the Hampton case: O'Reilly, 315.

Chapter Sixteen: The Specter

p. 158: "Boy, come here": quoted in Powers, *Secrecy and Power,* 411.

p. 159: "colored parents are not . . . cleanliness of their children": ibid., 330.

p. 159: "the specter of racial intermarriage": ibid., 329.

p. 159: "the latest form of the eternal rebellion against authority": ibid., 343.

p. 162: Hoover had kept up and modified his secret list: Theoharis and Cox, 172; Powers, *Secrecy and Power,* 337–338; and Tim Weiner, "Hoover Planned Mass Jailing in 1950," *New York Times,* December 23, 2007.

p. 162: COINTELPRO is discussed in all recent books on Hoover, the FBI, civil rights, and the confrontations of the 1960s, including Powers, *Secrecy and Power;* Powers, *Broken;* Gentry; and Theoharis and Cox.

p. 162: "twenty-thousand words of horror and infamy" and "exploded with rage": Fast, 350.

p. 163: "arrogant whipper-snapper . . . money and power": Roy Cohn describing Hoover's view of RFK, quoted in Schlesinger, 112. I talk about this same period and confrontation from Bobby Kennedy's point of view in my *Up Close: Robert F. Kennedy.* My understanding of Hoover has deepened and somewhat changed since I wrote that book, but the basic story remains the same.

p. 163: "runt": Lyndon Johnson quoted in Evan Thomas, *Robert Kennedy: His Life* (New York: Simon & Schuster, 2000), 32 and 365.

p. 165: To those who believe in conspiracies, Hoover's resistance to going after what we now call the Mafia is a clue as bright as a blazing sun: While rumors of Hoover's deals with the Mafia or of the blackmail evidence they had against him are widely available on the Internet, in YouTube videos taken from TV documentaries, and in books, responsible historians dismiss them. For Powers's assessment of the rumors, see *Broken,* 242 and 343, and *Secrecy and Power,* 564, footnote 41.

Chapter Seventeen: The Descent

p. 166: "Communist-inspired riot": quoted in Powers, *Secrecy and Power,* 351.

p. 166: "no less illegal . . . racial grounds": quoted in Johnson, 181.

p. 169: From the 1950s on, two brothers intimately involved . . . information to the Bureau: The inside information on the financing of the American Communist Party was first released to the public in Garrow, 35–43. For Garrow's most recent look at this material, see "The FBI and Martin Luther King," *The Atlantic Monthly,* vol. 290, no. 1 (July/August 2002), 80–88, http://www.theatlantic.com/past/docs/issues/2002/07/garrow.htm.

p. 171: "does not desire to be given . . . Communist Party": quoted in Garrow, 59.

p. 171: "I know Stanley . . . have to prove it": ibid., 61

p. 172: "I for one can't ignore the memos re King": ibid., 68.

p. 172: The excellent historian Richard Powers . . . everything his agents had been saying: Powers, *Broken,* 252.

p. 172: "I have certainly been misled . . . attached is correct": ibid., 252.

p. 172: "The Director is correct," "the most dangerous Negro . . . national security," and "It may be unrealistic . . . legalistic proofs": quoted in Garrow, 68–69.

p. 173: "I am glad you recognize . . . such influence": ibid., 74.

p. 173: "a fraud, demagogue, and moral scoundrel": quoted in Powers, *Broken,* 254.

p. 173: "I am glad that the 'light' . . . or wouldn't see it": quoted in Garrow, 106.

p. 173: It is not that devious Communists . . . civil rights movement: ibid., 99.

p. 174: "information developed regarding King's communist connections": ibid., 73.

p. 174: "neutralizing King as an effective Negro leader": ibid., 102.

p. 174: "expose King . . . first opportunity": ibid., 103.

p. 174: "destroy the burrhead": ibid., 106.

p. 176: "King, look into your heart . . . bared to the nation": ibid., 125–126.

p. 176: "they are out to break me": ibid., 134.

p. 176: "Every now and then . . . should be faithful to": ibid., 215.

p. 176: "It's a mixture . . . within each of us": ibid., 219.

Chapter Eighteen: COINTELPRO

p. 177: Between 1965 and 1967 . . . erupted in flames: Powers, *Secrecy and Power,* 422.

p. 178: "'neutralize' the effectiveness . . . liberation groups": quoted in Rosen, 241. Rosen's engaging history of the women's movement was aptly suggested to me by my neighbor and friend the historian Steven H. Jaffe. Any high-school student who wants to understand the changes in the lives of American women in the last half of the twentieth century will find this book both readable and informative.

p. 178: "should be viewed as . . . American values": ibid., 245–246.

p. 179: "shootings, beatings, and a high degree of unrest": quoted in U.S. Senate, *Final Report of the Select Committee to Study Government Operations with Respect to Intelligence Activities, Book III: Supplementary Detailed Staff Reports on Intelligence Activities and the Rights of Americans,* 94th Congress, 2nd sess., 1976, 192, Mary Ferrell Foundation website, http://www.maryferrell.org/mffweb/archive/viewer/showDoc.do?docId=1159&relPageId=198.

p. 179: "One of the interesting aspects . . . comb it out afterward": quoted in Rosen, 247.

p. 182: "mainly concerned with . . . any investigation" and "interwoven with its goals . . . achieve these goals": ibid., 245.

p. 182: In New York City, radical black nationalists . . . the government was responsible: Peter Blauner, "The Fugitive," *New York Magazine,* vol. 22, no. 31, (August 7, 1989), 34.

p. 182: Soviet agents, using tactics . . . Hoover's homosexuality: Andrew and Mitrokhin, 234–236. This is another book by a respected historian that makes use of files and contacts made available after the fall of Communism. Any student interested in the history of spying, or who wants to balance the picture of FBI deceptions with a sense of the operations of the Soviets, will find much to explore in it.

p. 184: "get the point across . . . every mailbox": quoted in Powers, *Secrecy and Power,* 466.

p. 186: wiretapping newspaper reporters: Theoharis and Cox, 413.

p. 186: tracking down who among them were homosexuals: ibid., 409.

p. 186: Tom Huston, an eager aide to Nixon . . . would be repealed: The Huston plan is discussed in any book on Nixon, Watergate, and this period in American history; for Hoover's reactions to it, see Theoharis and Cox, 417–423, or Powers, *Secrecy and Power,* 451–457.

p. 187: Presidents back to at least Herbert Hoover had requested illegal political invasions like this: Gentry, 152–153.

p. 189: "The United States must not adopt . . . important as ends": U.S. Senate, *Alleged Assassination Plots Involving Foreign Leaders: An Interim Report of the Select Committee to Study Government Operations with Respect to Intelligence Activities, Epilogue,* 94th Congress, 1st sess., 1975, Mary Ferrell Foundation website, http://www.maryferrell.org/mffweb/archive/docset/getList.do?docSetId=1014; quoted in Mayer, 28. This recent book is an indictment of our government's actions after 9/11. It shows how quickly and easily we returned to Hoover's policies and actions when we faced a new threat.

Epilogue: Master of Deceit, Then and Now

p. 192: those on the left insisted that McCarthy picked up men: Oshinsky, 310–311.

p. 192: those on the right spread questionable rumors about the Democrat Adlai Stevenson: Gentry, 402.

p. 192: Key court rulings in 1965 . . . because of their sexual orientation: Johnson, 202–209.

p. 193: Immediately after the September 11 attacks . . . no ties to terrorism: Morgan, 598.

p. 194: "The President could argue . . . had authorized it": Mayer, 152.

p. 196: "All life is an experiment," "in the competition of the market," and "be eternally vigilant . . . save the country": Abrams v. United States, 250 U.S. 616, November 10, 1919, FindLaw website, http://caselaw.lp.findlaw.com/scripts/getcase.pl?navby=search&court=US&case=/us/250/616.html.

BIBLIOGRAPHY

Ackerman, Kenneth D. *Young J. Edgar: Hoover, the Red Scare, and the Assault on Civil Liberties.* New York: Carroll & Graf, 2007.

Andrew, Christopher, and Vasili Mitrokhin. *The Sword and the Shield: The Mitrokhin Archive and the Secret History of the KGB.* New York: Basic Books, 1999.

Aronson, Marc. *Up Close: Robert F. Kennedy, a Twentieth-Century Life.* New York: Viking, 2007.

———. *Witch-Hunt: Mysteries of the Salem Witch Trials.* New York: Atheneum, 2003.

Bosworth, Patricia. *Anything Your Little Heart Desires: An American Family Story.* New York: Simon & Schuster, 1997.

Buhle, Paul, and Dave Wagner. *Blacklisted: The Film-Lover's Guide to the Hollywood Blacklist.* London: Palgrave, 2003.

Burrough, Bryan. *The Big Rich: The Rise and Fall of the Greatest Texas Oil Fortunes.* New York: Penguin, 2009.

Caute, David. *The Great Fear: The Anti-Communist Purge under Truman and Eisenhower.* New York: Simon & Schuster, 1978.

Charles, Douglas M. *J. Edgar Hoover and the Anti-interventionists: FBI Political Surveillance and the Rise of the Domestic Security State, 1939–1945.* Columbus: Ohio University Press, 2007.

Crossman, Richard H., ed. *The God That Failed.* London: Hamilton, 1950; reprint: New York: Columbia University Press, 2001.

Demaris, Ovid. *J. Edgar Hoover: As They Knew Him.* New York: Carroll & Graf, 1994.

Dufy, Susan, ed. *The Political Plays of Langston Hughes.* Carbondale: Southern Illinois University Press, 2000.

Fast, Howard. *Being Red.* Boston: Houghton Mifflin, 1990.

Felt, Mark, and John D. O'Connor. *A G-Man's Life: The FBI, Being "Deep Throat," and the Struggle for Honor in Washington.* New York: Public Affairs, 2007.

Finan, Christopher M. *From the Palmer Raids to the Patriot Act: A History of the Fight for Free Speech in America.* Boston: Beacon Press, 2007.

Gabler, Neal. *Winchell: Gossip, Power and the Culture of Celebrity.* New York: Vintage Books, 1994.

Garrow, David J. *The FBI and Martin Luther King, Jr.: From "Solo" to Memphis.* New York: Norton, 1981.

Gentry, Curt. *J. Edgar Hoover: The Man and the Secrets.* New York: Norton, 1991.

Goodman, James E. *Stories of Scottsboro.* New York: Pantheon, 1994.

Goodman, Walter. *The Committee: The Extraordinary Career of the House Committee on Un-American Activities.* New York: Farrar, Straus & Giroux, 1964.

Haynes, John Earl, Harvey Klehr, and Alexander Vassiliev. *Spies: The Rise and Fall of the KGB in America.* New Haven: Yale University Press, 2009.

Hoover, J. Edgar (William Sullivan and FBI Domestic Intelligence Division). *Masters of Deceit: The Story of Communism in America and How to Fight It.* New York: Henry Holt, 1958.

Jeffreys-Jones, Rhodi. *The FBI: A History.* New Haven: Yale University Press, 2007.

Johnson, David K. *The Lavender Scare: The Cold War Persecution of Gays and Lesbians in the Federal Government.* Chicago: University of Chicago Press, 2004.

Kaplan, Judy, and Linn Shapiro, eds. *Red Diapers: Growing Up in the Communist Left.* Chicago: University of Illinois Press, 1998.

Kazan, Elia. *A Life.* New York: Knopf, 1988.

Mayer, Jane. *The Dark Side: The Inside Story of How the War on Terror Turned Into a War on American Ideals.* New York: Doubleday, 2008.

Mendel, Arthur, ed. *Essential Works of Marxism.* New York: Bantam, 1961.

Miller, Arthur. *Timebends: A Life.* New York: Grove, 1987.

Morgan, Ted. *Reds: McCarthyism in Twentieth-Century America.* New York: Random House, 2003.

O'Reilly, Kenneth. *"Racial Matters": The FBI's Secret File on Black America, 1960–1972.* New York: Free Press, 1989.

Oshinsky, David M. *A Conspiracy So Immense: The World of Joe McCarthy.* New York: Free Press, 1983.

Powers, Richard Gid. *Broken: The Troubled Past and Uncertain Future of the FBI.* New York: Free Press, 2004.

———. *Secrecy and Power: The Life of J. Edgar Hoover.* New York: Free Press, 1987.

Proletarian Literature in the United States. New York: International Publishers, 1935.

Purvis, Alston W. *Vendetta: FBI Hero Melvin Purvis's War against Crime, and J. Edgar Hoover's War against Him.* New York: Public Affairs, 2005.

Rampersad, Arnold. *The Life of Langston Hughes.* Volume I: *1902–1941: I, Too, Sing America.* New York: Oxford University Press, 1986.

Reed, John. *Ten Days That Shook the World.* New York: Penguin, 1990.

Robins, Natalie. *Alien Ink: The FBI's War on Freedom of Expression.* New Brunswick, NJ: Rutgers University Press, 1992.

Rosen, Ruth. *The World Split Open: How the Modern Women's Movement Changed America.* New York: Viking, 2000.

Rosenfeld, Susan. "Doing Injustice to the FBI: The Negative Myths Perpetuated by Historians." *The Chronicle of Higher Education* 46, no. 7 (October 8, 1999): B6–B8.

Rosswurm, Steve. *The FBI and the Catholic Church, 1935–1962.* Amherst: University of Massachusetts Press, 2009.

Schlesinger, Arthur M., Jr. *Robert Kennedy and His Times.* New York: Ballantine Books, 1996.

Schrecker, Ellen. *The Age of McCarthyism: A Brief History with Documents.* New York: St. Martin's, 2002.

———. *Many Are the Crimes: McCarthyism in America.* Princeton, NJ: Princeton University Press, 1998.

Tanenhaus, Sam. *Whittaker Chambers: A Biography.* New York: Random House, 1998.

Theoharis, Athan G. *Abuse of Power: How Cold War Surveillance and Secrecy Policy Shaped the Response to 9/11.* Philadelphia: Temple University Press, 2011.

———, ed. *The FBI: A Comprehensive Reference Guide.* New York: Facts on File, 2000.

———, ed. *From the Secret Files of J. Edgar Hoover.* Chicago: Ivan R. Dee, 1991.

———. *J. Edgar Hoover, Sex, and Crime: An Historical Antidote.* Chicago: Ivan R. Dee, 1995.

———, and John Stuart Cox. *The Boss: J. Edgar Hoover and the Great American Inquisition.* Philadelphia: Temple University Press, 1988.

Tzouliadis, Tim. *The Forsaken: An American Tragedy in Stalin's Russia.* New York: Penguin, 2008.

Ungar, Sanford J. *FBI.* Boston: Little, Brown, 1976.

Weiner, Tim. *Legacy of Ashes: The History of the CIA.* New York: Random House, 2007.

Weinstein, Allen. *Perjury: The Hiss-Chambers Case.* New York: Knopf, 1978.

———, and Alexander Vassiliev. *The Haunted Wood: Soviet Espionage in America—the Stalin Era.* New York: Random House, 1999.

White, G. Edward. *Alger Hiss's Looking-Glass Wars.* New York: Oxford University Press, 2004.

Whitehead, Don. *The FBI Story: A Report to the People.* New York: Random House, 1956.

IMAGE CREDITS

p. iii: Courtesy of Universal Studios Licensing LLC. *You Can't Get Away with It!* copyright 1936 by Universal Pictures.

p. ix: Courtesy of Dr. David Garrow.

pp. x–1: Courtesy of the Tim Davenport collection.

p. 8: Courtesy of Réunion des Musées Nationaux / Art Resource, NY.

p. 12: National Archives, Records of the Federal Bureau of Investigation (FBI), Box 6, Folder 297.

p. 13: National Archives, FBI, Box 6, Folder 337.

p. 14: National Archives, FBI, Box 6, Folder 297.

p. 15: National Archives, FBI, Box 6, Folder 297.

p. 16: National Archives, FBI, Box 1, Folder 5.

p. 17: National Archives, FBI, Box 5, Folder 260.

p. 19: Library of Congress, Prints & Photographs Division, New York World-Telegram and the Sun Newspaper Photograph Collection, LC-USZ62-136235.

p. 21: Library of Congress, Prints & Photographs Division, LC-B2-5289-11.

p. 26: Courtesy of the Labadie Collection at the University of Michigan.

p. 28 (left): Cartoon from the *Chicago Tribune,* reprinted in *The Literary Digest,* June 28, 1919.

p. 28 (right): Cartoon from the *Brooklyn Eagle,* reprinted in *The Literary Digest,* November 15, 1919.

p. 31: Library of Congress, Prints & Photographs Division, LC-USZ62-75418.

p. 32: Library of Congress, Prints & Photographs Division, Harris & Ewing Collection, LC-H25-3316.

pp. 34–35: *Motion Picture Herald,* February 4, 1939, courtesy of University of Minnesota Special Collections.

p. 36: National Archives, FBI, Box 3, Folder 138.

p. 39: National Archives, FBI, Box 11, Folder 694.

p. 40: National Archives, FBI, Box 6, Folder 301.

p. 42: National Archives, FBI, Box 14, Folder 832.

p. 45 (top left): National Archives, FBI, Box 6, Folder 335.

p. 45 (top right): National Archives, FBI, Box 6, Folder 308.

p. 45 (bottom): National Archives, FBI, Box 8, Folder 431.

p. 46: National Archives, FBI, Box 14, Folder 846.

p. 47 (top): National Archives, FBI, Box 3, Folder 177.

p. 47 (bottom): National Archives, FBI, Box 14, Folder 874.

p. 49: Courtesy of Bettmann / Corbis / AP Images.

p. 53: Image courtesy of the National Archives, NWL-287-J1(14)11-D58.

p. 55: *Hollands, The Magazine of the South*, June 1936, courtesy of Post Toasties.

p. 56: National Archives, FBI, Box 5, Folder 272.

p. 57: National Archives, FBI, Box 4, Folder 215.

pp. 58–59: National Archives.

p. 60: Courtesy of Stork Club Enterprises.

p. 61: National Archives, FBI, Box 3, Folder 182

p. 62: Courtesy of Universal Studios Licensing LLC. *You Can't Get Away with It!* copyright 1936 by Universal Pictures.

p. 64 (top): PNational Archives, FBI, Box 10, Folder 628

p. 64 (bottom): National Archives.

p. 65 (top): National Archives, FBI, Box 5, Folder 246.

p. 65 (bottom): National Archives, FBI, Box 4, Folder 228.

p. 67: Photograph by Margaret Bourke-White, courtesy of the Masters Collection, Getty Images.

p. 68: Museum of Democracy.

p. 69: Courtesy of the Tim Davenport collection.

p. 71: National Archives, FBI, Box 3, Folder 146.

p. 72: National Archives, FBI, Box 1, Folder 59.

p. 73 (top): National Archives, FBI, Box 1, Folder 5.

p. 73 (bottom): National Archives, FBI, Box 14, Folder 849.

p. 75: Courtesy of MPI, Archive Photos Collection/Getty Images.

p. 77: Ilustration by William Hopper, courtesy of Craig Hopper, Library of Congress, LC-USZ62-43324.

p. 78: Courtesy of Otto Bettman/Corbis.

p. 79 (left): Courtesy of the Tamiment Library, New York University, Printed Ephemera Collection on Organizations, PE #036.

p. 79 (right): Courtesy of the Tamiment Library, New York University, Reference Center for Marxist Studies Pamphlet Collection, PE #043.

pp. 80–81: National Archives, FBI, Box 3, Folder 142.

p. 82: Courtesy of Doheny Memorial Library, Special Collections, University of Southern California.

p. 84: Courtesy of AP Images.

p. 86: National Archives, FBI, Box 4, Folder 206.

p. 88: Library of Congress, Prints & Photographs Division, New York World-Telegram and the Sun Newspaper Collection, LC-USZ62-111262.

p. 91: National Archives.

p. 92: National Archives, FBI, Box 6, Folder 339.

pp. 94–95: Photograph by Georgi Zelma, courtesy of the Hulton Archive/Getty Images.

p. 96: Courtesy of the David King Collection, London.

p. 98: Yurki Druzhnikov archives.

p. 100: National Archives, FBI, 208-NS-3848-2.

p. 105: National Archives, RG65-HM-11 Box 2.

p. 106: National Archives.

pp. 108–109: National Archives, 80-G-396229.

p. 110: Library of Congress, Prints & Photographs Division, New York-World Telegram and the Sun Newspaper Collection, LC-USZ62-122631.

p. 112: Radio Free Europe.

p. 115: Library of Congress, Prints & Photographs Division, New York World-Telegram and the Sun Newspaper Collection, LC-USZ62-117772.

p. 116: Library of Congress, Prints & Photographs Division, New York World-Telegram and the Sun Newspaper Collection, LC-USZ62-123068.

p. 119: Courtesy of MGM Media Licensing. *Kiss Me Deadly* copyright © 1955 by Metro-Goldwyn-Mayer Studios, Inc. All rights reserved.

p. 120: Courtesy of David Johnson.

p. 122 (right top and bottom): Courtesy of Otto Bettman/Corbis.

p. 124: Courtesy of the Margaret Chase Smith Library Collection.

p. 126: National Security Agency.

p. 128: Library of Congress, New York World-Telegram and the Sun Newspaper Collection, LC-USZ62-114977.

pp. 130–131: Courtesy of Universal Studios Licensing LLC. *Creature from the Black Lagoon* copyright 1954 by Universal Pictures Company.

p. 132: National Archives, FBI, Box 25, Folder 1414.

p. 134: National Archives, FBI, Box 8, Folder 488.

p. 135: National Archives, FBI, Box 25, Folder 1414.

p. 137: National Archives, FBI, Box 17, Folder 1123.

p. 138: Courtesy of the Robert Joyce Photography Collection, Historical Collections and Labor Archives, The Pennsylvania State University.

p. 143: Library of Congress, Prints & Photographs Division, New York World-Telegram & the Sun Newspaper Collection, LC-USZ62-119689.

p. 144: National Archives, FBI, Box 17, Folder 1128.

p. 145: Courtesy of AP Images.

p. 146: Courtesy of Columbia Pictures. *On the Waterfront* copyright 1954, renewed 1982 by Columbia Pictures Industries, Inc. All Rights Reserved.

p. 150: Library of Congress, Prints & Photographs Division, Look Magazine Photograph Collection, LC-USZ62-137206.

p. 152: National Archives, SEN 83A-B4.

pp. 154–155: Courtesy of the WFAA Collection, The Sixth Floor Museum at Dealey Plaza.

p. 156: Library of Congress, Prints & Photographs Division, U.S. News & World Report Magazine Collection, LC-U9-183B-20.

p. 158: National Archives.

p. 164: Courtesy of Ralph Crane / Time & Life Pictures / Getty Images.

p. 167: Courtesy of Barbara Gittings and Kay Tobin Lahusen Gay History Papers and Photographs, Manuscripts and Archives Division, The New York Public Library, Astor, Lenox and Tilden Foundations.

p. 169: Courtesy of Universal Studios Licensing LLC. *Spartacus* copyright © 1960 by Universal Pictures Company, Inc. & Bryna Productions, Inc.

p. 170: Photograph by Cecil Stoughton, courtesy of White House Photographs, John F. Kennedy Presidential Library and Museum, Boston.

p. 175: Courtesy of Dr. David Garrow.

p. 178: Library of Congress, Prints & Photographs Division, Yanker Poster Collection, LC-USZ62-91158.

p. 180 (top): Photograph by Warren K. Leffler, Library of Congress, Prints & Photographs Division, U.S. News & World Report Magazine Collection, LC-U9-18949-12.

p. 180 (bottom): Library of Congress, Yanker Poster Collection, LC-USZ62-123293.

p. 181 (top): National Archives, 111-SC-636742.

p. 181 (bottom): Photograph by John Filo, courtesy of the Premium Archive / Getty Images.

p. 182: Library of Congress, Yanker Poster Collection, LC-USZC4-2871.

p. 183: Students for a Democratic Society archive.

p. 184: *Win* Magazine, vol. 8, no. 5 (March 15, 1972), 8, courtesy of the Swarthmore College Peace Collection.

p. 185: National Archives, NLRN-WHPO-8146-03A.

p. 186: Library of Congress, Yanker Poster Collection, LC-DIG-yan-1a38772.

p. 188: Design by Philip Lief and Marcel Feigel, copyright © 1973 by Philip Lief. At the National Portrait Gallery, Smithsonian Institution. Library of Congress, Prints & Photographs Divison, Yanker poster collection, LC-USZ62-93125.

p. 194: Courtesy of John Emerson and Trevor Paglen.

p. 195: Image by Jonathan Landy, McClatchy Washington Bureau, Oct. 26, 2006, courtesy of TMS Reprints.

p. 197 (Louis Post): Library of Congress, Prints & Photographs Division, LC-USZ62-75418.

p. 197 (Dr. Martin Luther King Jr.): Photograph by Marion S. Trikosko, Library of Congress, Prints & Photographs Division, U.S. News & World Report Magazine Collection, LC-U9-11696-9A.

p. 197 (Margaret Chase Smith): Library of Congress, Prints & Photographs Division, LC-USZ62-42661.

p. 197 (Frank Kameny): Library of Congress, Frank Kameny Collection, Box 106, Folder 8.

Every effort has been made to obtain permission from the relevant copyright holders to ensure that all credits are correct. Any omissions are inadvertent and will be corrected in future editions if notification is given to the publishers in writing.

ACKNOWLEDGMENTS

This book has taken so long and been helped by so many hands that I have to divide the thank-yous into categories:

On the research side, my neighbor and reading group buddy Joe Dubek shared his experience of arriving at work at the World Trade Center on September 11, 2001, which, in earlier drafts, framed the book. I gained a great deal from lunchtime discussions with my historian-friend Dr. Steven Jaffe and was grateful for suggestions from Dr. Josh Brown; Dr. Leonard Cassuto generously shared many insights into 1950s film and fiction; Dr. David Garrow responded to my e-mail with generous aid, including the two versions of the King letter I have reprinted. In turn, he pointed me to one of the two expert readers who reviewed my manuscript.

I sent the manuscript to two academics for their comments. Both are excellent scholars who have read deeply in the primary sources and are on any list of FBI experts. One asked to remain anonymous; the other is Dr. Douglas M. Charles, whose work on Hoover and the anti-interventionists is listed in the source notes. The two letters I got back could not have been more different. In fact while each scholar made extensive, detailed, and helpful comments, outside of noticing a spelling error, their remarks had not one single observation in common.

The first expert reader was focused on what can be proven from primary sources and emphasized the ways in which Hoover functioned within the laws and expectations of his time. The expert strongly objected to the view that Hoover's personality quirks led him astray or that the FBI itself was characterized by racism or intrusive illegal actions. That reader recommended Athan Theoharis's *The FBI: A Comprehensive Reference Guide* as a more objective and nuanced view of the agency than is found in many books, even by accomplished historians. Dr. Charles, on the other hand, pointed to the most recent book by Dr. Theoharis, *Abuse of Power.* This latest study by the dean of FBI historians argues that Hoover claimed more authority than FDR actually gave him and mishandled the pursuit of Soviet spies because of his own obsessions. When two highly trained experts disagree so completely, when each cites work overseen by the same senior scholar but for entirely opposed reasons, it is clear that the study of Hoover and the FBI is still charged and contentious. But it was wonderful for me to get such informed and helpful advice, and my book is better for it.

Several people who have written about the FBI responded to my e-mails. I was grateful to Sam Tanenhaus, editor of the *New York Times Book Review,* for giving me his insights into the Cold War and the Hiss trials, and to Dr. Ellen Schrecker, Dr. Aaron Purcell, Dr. Kim Phillips-Fein, and Kenneth Ackerman for general encouragement and suggested readings.

Of course, and I underline this, everything in this book is the product of my research and represents my own judgment. The fact that others read it in whole, in part, or in earlier drafts does not imply they agree with, or are responsible for, anything I say.

As I was writing the book, I sent it out to several teachers and teenagers to read. Larry Jones gave me the chance to present its main argument to teachers in Glendale, California. I owe a great debt to Hayden Baker-Kline, a brilliant high-school student, who read two different versions and sent back the most extensive and helpful editorial notes. Knowing that readers like Hayden are out there inspires me to write my books.

Thanks to Ken Wright for shepherding this project through the wilds of publishing, and to everyone at Candlewick Press for believing in it. Especially to Liz Bicknell and Carter Hasegawa for the editorial queries that made the book so much better; to Hannah Mahoney for such careful notes; and to Renée Cafiero. Renée's copyediting comments were not only useful but personal—she knew Frank Kameny "back in the day." I'm also grateful to Amy Berniker for taking my design suggestions seriously and going one better with the book, and to Pam Consolazio for inventing such a compelling cover. Carter, working way overtime, and the invaluable Michael Cooper—with a special assist from my friend John W. Glenn—were my saviors in the last days of photo research; we would not have the richly illustrated book I always wanted without them. My colleagues and students in the Rutgers University School of Communication and Information have created a nurturing home for intellectual freedom which was just the right place to finish writing this book.

Thanks to my wife, Marina Budhos, for reading the whole book in two very different incarnations and, as ever, helping me to find the best words, and to Sasha and Rafi for putting up with a dad who was forever disappearing into his office, his books, and the past. And finally to my mother and (long ago) my father, who lived through this entire period of history and gave me their insights—from my father's distaste for the Communists during the 1917 revolution, to his experiences among the devout leftists of the Group Theater, to my mother's memories of her sister's troubles after the war, to my parents' shared time of working with close friends suffering from the blacklist in the 1950s, to the heroism of Arthur Miller—their tales made this vast political drama of Left and Right into the personal stories of individual human beings. I hope some of that comes through on these pages.

INDEX

Bold page numbers indicate images or captions. The initials JEH in subheadings refer to J. Edgar Hoover.